G000274523

Classical Buildings of Wiltshire & Bath

A Palladian Quest

Classical Buildings of Wiltshire & Bath

A Palladian Quest

Richard Durman

Millstream Books

above: Amesbury Abbey
frontispiece: Belcombe Court, Bradford-on-Avon. (© Crown copyright, N.M.R.)
title-page illustration: Venetian window, No.24 High Street, Warminster

First published in 2000 by Millstream Books, 18 The Tyning, Widcombe, Bath BA2 6AL

Set in Palatino and printed in Great Britain by The Amadeus Press, Cleckheaton, West Yorkshire

ISBN 0948975601

A catalogue record for this book is available from the British Library

Contents

List of Abbreviations used in the text

Colvin	A reference to *A Biographical Dictionary of British Architects 1600-1840* by Howard Colvin (Murray, London, 1954; new edition 1978).
DoE	(Department of the Environment) A reference to the relevant official list of buildings of special architectural or historical interest.
Ison	A reference to *The Georgian Buildings of Bath* by Walter Ison (Faber & Faber, London, 1948; reprinted Kingsmead Press, Bath, 1980).
RCHM	The Royal Commission on the Historical Monuments of England.
Pevsner	A reference to either the Wiltshire volume (1975 edition, revised by Bridget Cherry) or the North Somerset and Bristol volume (1958), as appropriate, of *The Buildings of England* series by Nikolaus Pevsner.
Summerson	A reference to *Architecture in Britain 1530-1830* by John Summerson (Penguin Books, Harmondsworth, 1953, 5th revised edition, 1969).
Worsley	A reference to *Classical Architecture in Britain, The Heroic Age* by Giles Worsley (Yale University Press, New Haven & London, 1995).

Preface

I have enjoyed seeking out Wiltshire and Bath's rich heritage of classical architecture though it has felt something of an act of self-indulgence. Concentrating on the architectural forms of buildings of the 17th and 18th centuries allows us to skip lightly through the era, gazing at what pleases us and ignoring the less happy aspects of life in those times. For what we shall be looking at, in the main, are buildings built either for the rich or for the very rich. It is difficult to ignore the fact that much of the wealth for these expensive building projects came from landed or commercial assets worked either by people earning derisory wages or, in the colonies, by slave labour. We shall see, for example, how many who built homes in Wiltshire did so on the strength of profits made from the sugar plantations of Jamaica. Even the Reverend Mr.Horlock of Box was able to build Box House (now a hotel) as his retirement home in 1790 with the wealth he had derived from that source. This is not to say, of course, that there were only two tiers of society, the haves and the have-nots. Subtle stratifications were emerging and, as Voltaire had observed, it was possible in England, unlike in France, for a man to raise his social status through his own efforts; this was well-exemplified in the business of building where, as we shall see, a lowly social origin was not a bar to becoming an eminent architect.

Another danger is that we attach far more importance to the subtleties of building design than did the people for whom the buildings were actually designed. This was, after all, the world depicted by Defoe, Fielding, Hogarth and others in which most people's lives were driven by wordly ambition, the quest for greater power or wealth, or simply by a craving for pleasure and excitement. How many, in truth, really cared about architecture as opposed to the purely practical aspects of the buildings they needed to use? Apart from the fact that architecture was a topic of interest only to a limited élite, it was regarded as something that only applied to buildings of some prestige. The poor did not live in 'architecture' except as servants in quarters that would today be condemned as insanitary. In the countryside, the poor lived in simple cottages, for the most part in squalid and overcrowded conditions that their social 'betters' would not begin to recognise as a disgrace until well into the 19th century. Of course there were a few random acts of charity and a growing sense of duty in a few patrician breasts towards the 'ordinary people'. But it was only towards the end of the 18th century that, through a sense of humanity for humanity's sake, there start to appear a few well-built estate cottages, a few well-designed almshouses and even infirmaries for the sick – although, in our area, there was only one, in Salisbury, that was built for the population at large and another, in Bath, to cater for the deserving poor who might benefit from taking the waters.

None of the ancient or Renaissance writers from whom the Palladian architects drew their inspiration had anything to say about houses for the general population – or, at any rate, about how they should be *designed*. Their design advice was limited to public buildings and to houses for the ruling or wealthy classes; Alberti does have a few words of advice about designing for "middling people" (whose houses should imitate those of the rich "but with such Moderation, as not to run into a greater Expense than they can well support") but that is as far as he goes. It is not that their worlds did not provide for the poor, it was just that they did not regard 'architecture' as having anything to do with the lower classes of society – an attitude that would have been largely shared by the gentlemen of the 17th and 18th centuries.

Special thanks are due to my publisher, Tim Graham, for all his support and encouragement. I am also very grateful to the building conservation officers of all six District or Unitary Councils for their generosity in giving me their time and ideas especially in relation to the matters discussed in the last two chapters (I am conscious the greatest burden fell on David McLaughlin of Bath & North East Somerset); to the staff of the Building of Bath Museum, the Wiltshire & Swindon Record Office and the Wiltshire Education & Libraries Department, especially Duncan Coe of the Archaeology Service and Bruce Purvis, Salisbury's Local Studies Librarian, for his interest and assistance.

1 Introduction

The Buildings and the Architects

Stonehenge, Avebury, Salisbury Cathedral – these are Wiltshire's best known memorials and buildings. But Wiltshire is also a very special area for anyone interested in that refined style of classicism that we call Palladian, first introduced into England by Inigo Jones in the 17th century and strongly revived early in the next. This revival coincided with the beginning of the rapid rise of the neighbouring city of Bath to the heights of fame and fashion and it comes as no surprise that the predominant style of its buildings is Palladian. So between them Wiltshire and Bath amassed – 'hogged', perhaps – far more than their fair share of Palladian building endeavour.

This book is intended as a guide to those buildings (or to a large selection of them, at any rate) but will not deal with Palladianism in isolation from other forms of classicism. For one thing, 'Palladianism' is not easy to pin down. The period between Inigo Jones and the Palladian Revival is full of examples of buildings which some commentators would call 'Palladian' but others would insist were not. Similarly, a wider range of neo-classical styles were developed as the 18th century went on and the 19th century began and opinions will differ as to whether a particular building is Palladian or neo-classical. The distinctions are usually too subtle to worry about. What is important is that early in the 18th century an approach to building design became established which was 'classical' and unashamedly academic. Another reason for not taking too narrow a view is that the nature of Palladianism is probably better understood by looking at examples of the full range of classical forms that can be seen in Wiltshire and Bath. For this reason, the 'shape' of this book will be rather like a rugby ball – fat in the middle (when it is dealing with Palladian buildings) and tapering each side (when it is covering the early stages of classicism and, on the other side, the later stages of classical architecture). The term 'Georgian' is a useful one – and will be used a great deal – since the span of the consecutive reigns of George I to George IV (1714-1830) neatly covers the period between the first stirrings of the Palladian Revival and the eventual demise of classicism as the most widely acceptable architectural style in Britain. Yet it cannot serve as the exclusive agenda for this book as the term excludes the work of Inigo Jones and his school even though most of us would be hard pressed to distinguish their works from Georgian buildings.

So what is there still to be seen? In Wiltshire, some buildings have disappeared (notably, Fonthill Splendens) and some have changed beyond all recognition (Wilbury Manor, Tottenham House); in Bath, the number of

Georgian buildings that have been lost through rebuilding, bombing or post-war redevelopment would be enough to fill a small township (Wilton, say). But, within our area, a satisfyingly large number remain. Just the list of Palladian or neo-classical country houses that are open to the public is an impressive one – Bowood House, Lydiard Tregoze, Philipps House, Pythouse, Stourhead House and Wilton House. At Prior Park, although public access extends only to the grounds (including the Palladian Bridge), this is sufficient to appreciate the siting and design of Ralph Allen's noble mansion on the edge of Bath. Corsham Court, a house with an unusually complex architectural history, includes elements of 18th-century classicism. Many fine Georgian buildings are still in active public use and can normally be visited on most days of the week. Examples in Bath are the Great Pump Room, the New Assembly Rooms, the Guildhall, the Holburne Museum and, on its eastern fringe, Claverton Manor which contains the American Museum.

The urban delights of Bath are well known but Bradford-on-Avon, Chippenham, Devizes, Marlborough, Salisbury, Trowbridge and Warminster all have much to offer to anyone who enjoys 18th-century townscape. It is not only town houses of the Georgian period that will be reviewed here but also hotels, hospitals, churches, public halls and prisons.

Last come the more elusive, less accessible beauties scattered around the countryside of Wiltshire or on the fringes of its towns. One is a great house of monumental presence, Wardour Castle (the 'new' 18th-century house, not to be confused with the adjoining medieval Old Wardour Castle) and Amesbury Abbey, in terms of stateliness, comes close behind. And then there are smaller gems like Trafalgar House, Belcombe Court and Bowden Park House.

Just as remarkable is the large number of distinguished architects whose work is represented in Bath and Wiltshire. There is surely no other area of Britain of comparable size (outside London) that can boast of surviving buildings by so many of the leading architects of their age – Inigo Jones, Richard Boyle (3rd Earl of Burlington), Colen Campbell, Henry Flitcroft, John Wood the Elder, John Wood the Younger, James Paine, Sir Robert Taylor, Robert Adam, Sir William Chambers, James Wyatt, George Dance the Younger, Sir Jeffry Wyatville and Sir John Soane. Possibly less well known than these, though with a distinguished national reputation are John Webb, Sir William Benson, John James, Henry Herbert (9th Earl of Pembroke), Roger Morris, Henry Keene, Nathaniel Ireson, John Vardy, Samuel Pepys Cockerell, George Steuart, Sanderson Miller and Nicholas Revett. In addition, Bath owes its present character to a group of architects who did little or no work outside Bath, or, in some cases, Bath and Bristol. But there are two in this group, Thomas Baldwin and John Pinch, whose contribution to the buildings of Bath is so important that it seems unfortunate that their influence beyond the city was minimal, though the likely reason for this will appear in later chapters.

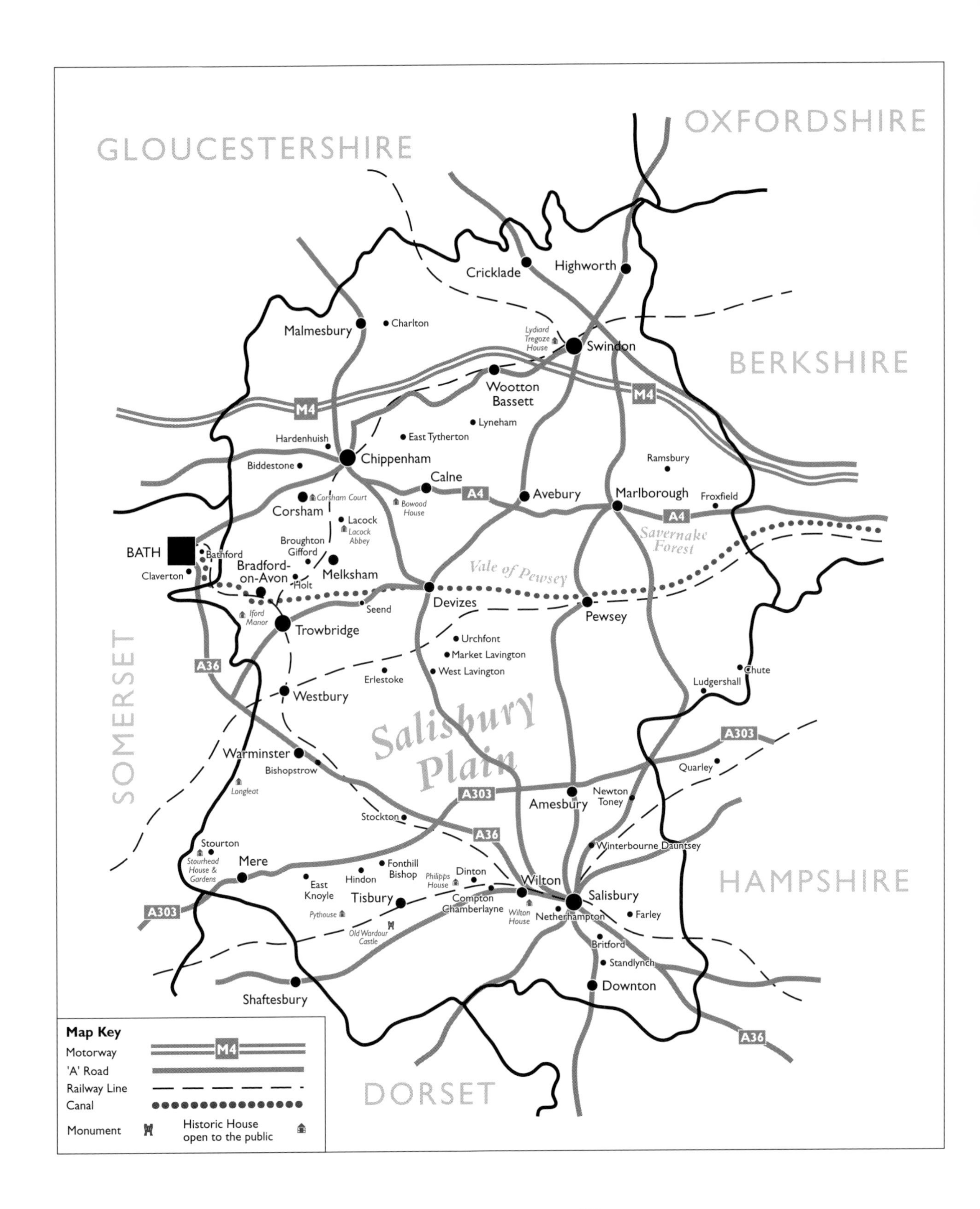
GLOUCESTERSHIRE
OXFORDSHIRE
BERKSHIRE
HAMPSHIRE
SOMERSET
DORSET
Cricklade
Highworth
Malmesbury
Charlton
Lydiard Tregoze House
Swindon
M4
Wootton Bassett
Lyneham
East Tytherton
Hardenhuish
Chippenham
Biddestone
Ramsbury
Calne
A4
Avebury
Marlborough
Froxfield
Corsham Court
Corsham
Bowood House
Lacock
Lacock Abbey
Savernake Forest
BATH
Bathford
Broughton Gifford
Claverton
Bradford-on-Avon
Holt
Melksham
Vale of Pewsey
Devizes
Pewsey
Seend
Iford Manor
Trowbridge
Urchfont
Market Lavington
West Lavington
A36
Erlestoke
Chute
Ludgershall
Westbury
Salisbury Plain
A303
Warminster
Bishopstrow
Quarley
Longleat
Amesbury
Newton Toney
Stockton
Stourton
Winterbourne Dauntsey
Stourhead House & Gardens
Mere
Fonthill Bishop
Hindon
Dinton
Philipps House
East Knoyle
Tisbury
Wilton
Salisbury
Compton Chamberlayne
Pythouse
Wilton House
Netherhampton
Farley
Old Wardour Castle
Britford
Standlynch
Downton
Shaftesbury
Map Key
Motorway
'A' Road
Railway Line
Canal
Monument
Historic House open to the public

The Area

The linking of Wiltshire and Bath requires an explanation, perhaps, since Bath does not actually lie within that county. Until 1974, Bath lay within Somerset; it then formed part of Avon until that county ceased to exist in 1996 and is now back within Somerset though with 'unitary' status as part of a larger area called Bath & North East Somerset. The former City of Bath retains its status as such through the adoption of the system of charter trustees which allows, for example, for the election of a Mayor for the City alongside the position of Chairman of the District Council.

A look at the map opposite shows that whereas Bath & North East Somerset shares a boundary with Wiltshire, the City of Bath does not. It is separated from Wiltshire by that glorious stretch of the Avon valley that runs north/south from Batheaston to Limpley Stoke and contains the parishes of Batheaston, Bathampton, Bathford, Claverton and Monkton Combe. The Wiltshire boundary actually crosses the Avon briefly, south of the Dundas Aqueduct, to follow the line of the Wellow Brook, as if the county were making a bid to encircle Bath from the south before thinking better of it and darting back eastwards to Limpley Stoke and Freshford. 'Wiltshire and Bath' was a European Parliamentary constituency until 1999 when Regions and proportional representation made constituencies redundant. Bath has a strong magnetic attraction across the western and northern parts of Wiltshire, serving as a choice shopping centre for people who live in those parts and a desirable place to live for people who work in them.

In coaching days the vast majority of journeys within the northern and central parts of the county were to or from Bath along the various roads to London with the next strongest link between Salisbury and Bath (see fig.1). There were several routes between Bath and London and they changed from time to time as the road system delevoped, but, in outline, coming from the London direction, they all went through Marlborough and, a few miles further west, Beckhampton (near Avebury); there was then a choice of a northern route through Chippenham or a southern route through Devizes.[1]

1. The latter route was evidently the one used by 'Mr.Simkin B_N_R_D' in Christopher Anstey's satirical *New Bath Guide* of 1766 ("What tho' at Devizes I felt pretty hearty / And made a good meal, like the rest of the party ...").

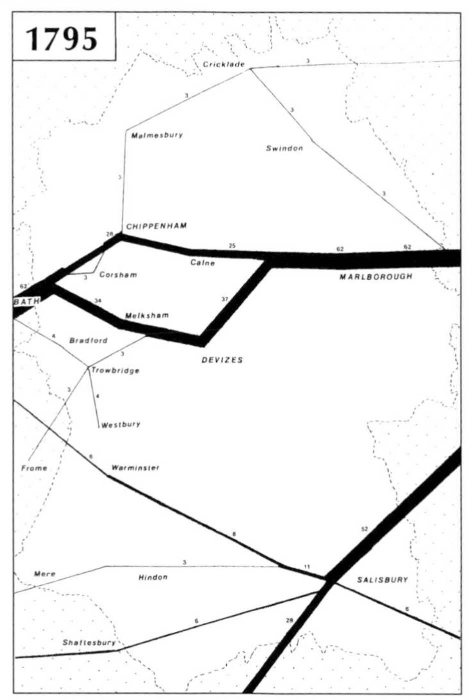

1. *Diagram of the number of stagecoaches (including mailcoaches) travelling in one direction in 1795. The figures are approximate as the directory on which they are based appeared at intervals between 1790 and 1798 (see* Stagecoach Operation Through Wiltshire *by John H. Chandler for South Wiltshire Archaeological Society, 1980).*
(John Chandler)

Of course, the coach services on these routes were there principally to take those seeking the waters and social delights of Bath from London and back again. Nevertheless they enabled freer and easier intercourse to take place between Bath on the one hand and Marlborough, Calne, Chippenham and Devizes, for example, on the other. It is interesting that in the *Victoria County History of Wiltshire* (vol.4) a map showing the development of turnpike roads in Wiltshire after 1700 treats Bath as if it were part of the county.

The early years of the 19th century saw the opening of the Kennet and Avon Canal with Bradford-on-Avon assuming a new importance and becoming closer to Bath in a way that it had never done before despite its geographical proximity. The canal also provided easier transport of goods to and from Devizes as evidenced by the greater use of Bath stone (rather than local brick) in buildings put up after the arrival of the canal.[2] With the coming of the railways, the links with Wiltshire were further strengthened with the Bath/London line running through Chippenham and Swindon and the Bath/Salisbury line running through Bradford-on-Avon, Trowbridge, Westbury, Warminster and (until the closure of the station in the Beeching era) Wilton. Furthermore, for a hundred years or so, though becoming now a distant memory, a line ran roughly due east from Bath through Devizes and Pewsey and on to Hungerford, in Berkshire, and beyond. The building of the M4 across the north of Wiltshire is probably insignificant in terms of links with Bath, because it lies so far to the north, but the steady improvement of the A36 trunk road between Southampton and Bristol has made the journey between Bath and Salisbury both quicker and easier.

A study of buildings, such as Pevsner's *The Buildings of England*, undertaken on a county by county basis, is necessarily tied by the boundaries of the various counties according to whatever they might be at the time of the study. The present study need not be so confined and gives the reader the benefit of seeing as a whole an area of Britain which is remarkable for the reasons spelt out in the first part of this chapter.

Most of the buildings considered in this book lie within an area formed by joining up Marlborough, Salisbury, Shaftesbury, Bath and Chippenham. This does not mean that Swindon or its rural hinterland will be ignored – Lydiard Tregoze and Highworth are both of special interest – but Swindon itself has only come to prominence since the railway age and few of its buildings are able to qualify for attention here. ('Swindon', the former 'Thamesdown', now has unitary status, but is treated here as forming part of Wiltshire geographically.) Cricklade and Wootton Bassett will also feature here.

2. Though, ironically, the digging of the Caen Hill locks on the west side of Devizes led to the discovery of the largest deposit of Gault clay – excellent for making bricks – that had been found in England at that time and, while the bed lasted, Devizes benefited from a prosperous brick-making industry as a result.

The Geology

The appearance of the buildings of a particular region is strongly influenced by the materials available. The situation in Bath and Wiltshire is not as complex as it might be having regard to the bewilderingly fast geological changes that can occur during the course of a journey across Britain (making Britain's scenery as changeable as its weather). Even so, what follows deliberately concentrates on the more important features and omits some of the finer detail. The whole of the north and west of Wiltshire and the whole of Bath lie within the band of oolitic limestone that runs in a great arc across England between Portland and Whitby passing through the Cotswolds and Northamptonshire. The best of the building stone here is called 'Bath' stone and during the 18th century most of it came from Ralph Allen's quarries on Combe Down or from neighbouring Bathampton Down; but most of the quarries that supplied it lie in Wiltshire. Some towns in north Wiltshire – Highworth, Wootton Bassett and Calne – are built of a similar, but coarser, oolitic limestone. 'Limestone' means stone composed primarily of the compressed skeletal remains of creatures that lived in the sea about 140 to 195 million years ago. 'Oolitic' means that it consists of rounded grains like the hard roe of a herring.

Most of the remainder of Wiltshire, in the east and south, also contains limestone, but in this case chalk, laid down about 70 to 140 million years ago. For this is the region of Wiltshire's chalk hills running into Berkshire in the north-east, into Hampshire to the east and south-east and into Dorset from its south-west corner. The use of chalk as a building material is rarely found outside 'vernacular' buildings in the countryside; but where there is chalk there is invariably flint (or silica) which is indestructible as a building material and has therefore been used a great deal within the chalk areas – either in its original 'lumpy' form or after it has been split ('knapped') to give a shiny dark appearance. Locally, this is either black or dark grey.

Finally, between these two great areas of different limestones lies a relatively narrow band of sandstone (i.e. compressed sand) known as greensand. Greensand is always found alongside chalk but it is best visualised here as running alongside the band of oolitic limestone but forming a salient by plunging off eastwards down into the Pewsey Vale. It does not wear as well as most forms of limestone but was used, for example, for the original Tudor house at Wilton. It was used in Salisbury's very first Cathedral at Old Sarum but the Cathedral at New Sarum, begun in 1220, was built in a limestone from Chilmark and Tisbury.[3] This came from quarries which constitute an outlier of the Portland beds to the south (though with a higher content of sand than true Portland stone) and is the one major exception to the simple triptych of oolitic limestone-greensand-chalk.

3. Recent research shows that although the stone for the Victorian restoration of the Cathedral was taken from underground quarries in Chilmark, the stone for the original building probably came from seams nearer the surface in and around Tisbury.

2. *18th-century house at Avebury built of sarsen stone.*

The only other relevant geological features to mention are the presence of clay deposits at various sites in the areas of chalk and greensand and the presence of sarsens (or 'grey wethers') on the chalk downs between Devizes and Marlborough. These are what remain of a crust of hard sandstone that overlay the chalk hereabouts. They were the stones used for the building of Avebury but many were broken up and re-used (fig.2).

These geological characteristics proved very significant in the Georgian era when elegance and refinement were the desiderata. In Bath and other places with good access to the limestone quarries the creamy-coloured Bath stone was the natural and happy choice. It is a good freestone – that is to say, it can be carved in any direction – and is eminently suitable for producing smooth-faced, or 'ashlar', blocks for façades. The principal disadvantages proved to be its porosity (necessitating blocks many inches thick on faces exposed to the wind and rain) and the readiness with which it turned black and lost its naturally warm appearance in the soot-laden atmosphere of the 19th and 20th centuries. In Bath, most of the sooty deposits have been removed but, where they have been allowed to remain, the contrast is clear to see. Where stone was less easily available, the choice of material for Georgian buildings was brick. In the Age of Elegance, neither chalk nor flint were ever likely to be serious candidates for houses aspiring to architectural quality (though a few examples of Georgian buildings faced with flint do exist in other parts of England, notably in Sussex). Nearly all the brick used would have been produced locally from the clay deposits that have been mentioned. The dark red bricks of Devizes, for example, were very different from the yellowy/ grey bricks that were made and used in Salisbury.[4] Except in the most modest dwellings, brick would normally be used in association with stone dressings, for example around doors and windows, on the corners and for bands or string courses between storeys (see figs.3 & 4).

3. Houses in Kingsbury Square, Wilton, with and without stone dressings.

The effect that the use of different building materials can have on the character both of individual buildings and on a whole town (or village) cannot be overstated. This is dramatically shown by comparing Bath and Marlborough. The creamy-coloured stone of Bath is, of course, what gives the city its character above all else but, because it has been used so extensively and its terraces have been designed in such a consistent fashion, it is actually possible to tire of it if taken in too large a dose. A visit to Marlborough would be the ideal means of refreshment. For it is a town built almost entirely of brick, and very fine brick too. The various shades of red and 'burnt' (or, more strictly, 'over-burnt') blue give a sparkle and charm in complete contrast to the smooth elegance of Bath stone.

Away from these two extremes, there is greater variety in the appearance of buildings in the other towns of Wiltshire – though there is little in Bradford-on-Avon that is not built of Bath stone. The 18th century buildings of both Chippenham and Trowbridge are predominantly of Bath stone and there is

4. Most Georgian buildings in Salisbury, however, are of red brick, coming in part perhaps from the two brickyards that operated in Downton in those days.

4. A rich mix of brick and Bath stone at No.8 High Street, Devizes (1737)

a great deal of it to be found both in Devizes and, more surprisingly in view of its distance from the band of oolitic limestone, Warminster. In Salisbury, brick predominates with some of the more prestigious houses in the Cathedral Close in Chilmark stone. Bath stone was not used in Salisbury in any significant way until the 19th century. By then, the railways enabled building materials to be transported further and more cheaply, and clients and their architects had a wider choice. In Castle Street in Salisbury, for example, stand two Edwardian buildings (at the junction with Chipper Lane) which incorporate Portland stone from Dorset, Ham Hill stone from Somerset and granite from Cornwall. Nowadays, such is the wide choice and availability of building materials from all over the world that it is often no longer the cheapest option to use local materials. The visual character of an area is often only maintained through local development control policies requiring the use of traditional materials.

2 Classicism and the Italian Renaissance

'Classicism' has several meanings but there are only two of relevance to building design. The first is a general one (which need not detain us long) referring not so much to a 'style' as to what has been described as "an ideal derived from the past ... an aesthetic based on the idea of refined plainness".[1] The second meaning is a more specific one that applies to Western architecture and design (and so is the one with which we are more concerned). Classicism in architecture is a reference to a style that is based on the forms of the buildings of ancient Rome (which were, as we shall see, originally regarded as subsuming those of ancient Greece) conveyed to us originally through their 're-discovery' at the time of the Italian Renaissance (in the 15th and 16th centuries) and later more directly through the study of ancient buildings of the Roman world and, later still, those of ancient Greece. (What those 'forms' consist of will be looked at more closely in the next chapter.)

It is remarkable enough that a style of architecture developed and refined in central Italy in the first two centuries BC should have held sway throughout the vast Roman Empire as it expanded over the next 500 years. What is, perhaps, even more remarkable is that Roman architecture should receive a fresh lease of life a thousand years after the sack of Rome and then, for the next 400 years, become the standard design style for building across the western world (in Britain's case, only for the last 300 of those 400 years for reasons we shall see later).

The scholars of the Italian Renaissance in the 15th century were the first to rediscover, in a systematic way, the wisdom of 'the ancients'. This term referred exclusively to the ancient Romans; the achievements of the somewhat earlier Greek civilisation were, at that time, seen only through the eyes of the Romans, so to speak. (The arts, sciences and philosophies of Greece were not studied in their own right until well into the 18th century.) The Renaissance was also about Humanism[2] and the idea of the Universal Man (*uomo universale*) with knowledge of the sciences of arithmetic, geometry, astronomy and music and with skill in arts like painting. Architecture was seen, not so much as an art, but as a science closely related to the others. This was because it was believed that from those sciences could be derived measurable proportions and ratios and that these could, in turn, be reflected in architecture.

What is slightly confusing is that the earliest, and among the best known, buildings that we now recognise as belonging to the Renaissance owed very little, in fact, to Roman architecture. The Foundling Hospital in Florence,

1. Michael Greenhalgh in *What is Classicism?* (Academy Editions, London, 1990)
2. At the time, the term meant only the study of Roman and Greek literature; Humanism in its current sense derived from the interpretation of the Renaissance by later generations.

for example, by Filippo Brunelleschi (1377-1446) is generally regarded as the first example of Renaissance architecture but its forms derive far more from those of traditional Tuscan Romanesque than those of Imperial Rome. Brunelleschi's Duomo in Florence is often described as Renaissance in its construction methods but Gothic in spirit. But his later buildings contained more Roman details and, by the end of his career, he could be regarded as much a neo-classicist as those that followed him.

So what had happened? As more Roman texts were dusted off and studied, the architects of the age became frustrated that none of them related to building construction and design. It was only in 1414 that a manuscript at St.Gall, in Switzerland, was recognised as being exactly that. It had been written by an obscure Roman architect, Vitruvius, who lived in the 1st century AD; the work, *De Architectura,* consisted of ten chapter-length treatises that would soon be referred to as the *Ten Books on Architecture* in which Vitruvius set down what he believed were the governing principles of architecture. It is at times a difficult, confusing and often tedious work[3] but it had enormous influence because it was the only one of its kind ever found. He emphasised Harmony, Ratio, Proportion, Rhythm, Symmetry and Order (in its special architectural sense) – all with particular reference to the human body. The well-known image by Leonardo da Vinci of a man's body with outstretched arms standing within a square and a circle is one of a number of attempts at that time to illustrate a concept that Vitruvius had described in words in Chapter I of Book III ("If a man be placed flat on his back, with his hands and feet extended, and a pair of compasses centred at his navel ...").

The proportions of the face and the body were all regarded as highly significant and of value in the design of buildings. Based on Vitruvius, a philosophy of architecture evolved during the Italian Renaissance which can be summarised as follows – Man is in the image of God; the proportions of his body are produced by divine will; so the proportions of architecture must embrace and express the cosmic order. It is difficult to take this seriously today and, even in the 18th century, not only would Hogarth and others have great fun with it but philosophers like Hume and Burke would seek to refute that beauty had anything to do with calculation and geometry. Yet it all had a profound effect on the thinking and the work of the Renaissance architects.

The first to grasp the Vitruvian torch was Leone Battista Alberti (1404-1472). He was a true Renaissance man of many accomplishments and wrote about architecture more than he practised it. His few surviving buildings are important enough (as regards pointing the way as to how the Roman way of building could be adapted to contemporary needs) but it was his treatise *De Re Aedificatoria* (1452, fully published 1485) that made him such an influential

3. In his *Ten Books of Architecture* Leone Battista Alberti says that Vitruvius wrote "in such a manner that to the Latins he seems to write Greek, and to the the Greeks, Latin: But indeed it is plain from the Book itself, that he wrote neither Greek nor Latin, and he might almost as well have never wrote at all, at least with Regard to us, since we cannot understand him" (Book VI, Chapter I, Leoni Edition 1755).

figure.[4] The next important practitioner was Donato Bramante (1444-1514). He followed Vitruvian principles but, like Alberti (or indeed any great architect), did not merely copy what had already been done but produced his own unique creations which would themselves be an inspiration to others.

Meanwhile, other architects came along whom we now call Mannerists, that is to say, who were well-versed in the Vitruvian principles but did not believe that it was necessary to follow them slavishly. The principal early proponents of Mannerism were Giulio Romano (?-1546) and Michelangelo (1475-1564). They used the basic Roman vocabulary but were not prepared to follow the 'rules' as to how it should be used. They introduced features unknown to the Romans: giant columns and pilasters, the use of rustication on a massive scale, and pediments, cornices and other parts of a building treated in a sculptural way to produce a sense of swagger and freedom. They applied as much care and attention to breaking the rules as Alberti or Serlio, for example, did in trying to follow them.

The next after Alberti to produce an important written work was Sebastiano Serlio (1475-1554). This was *L'Architettura*, an assemblage of eight books of which six were published in his lifetime from 1537 onwards. The first, and only, English edition was published in 1611. It contained designs and became the most important source book until Palladio (though a close second, after it was published in England in 1669, was Vignola's *Regola delli Cinque Ordini d'Architettura* (1562)). Serlio paid the greatest compliment to Bramante by including an illustration of his Tempietto alongside samples of Roman architecture as an equally worthy exemplar.

But the most famous of the proponents of the Vitruvian principles was Andrea Palladio who was born in Padua in 1508 and died in 1580. He took the study of actual Roman buildings very seriously and produced a guide book to the antiquities of Rome which remained the best of its kind for travellers for about 200 years. His most influential buildings were to prove to be the villas he built in and around Vicenza (near Venice, in the region called Veneto, or, often, 'the Veneto') and his most important written work *The Four Books of Architecture (I Quattro Libri dell'Architettura*) in which he sought to apply the principles of Vitruvius to 16th-century Italy. In view of the influence this work was to have and the intensity with which it has been studied over the intervening centuries, it is, perhaps, worth looking very briefly at what *I Quattro Libri* actually say.

In Book I, Palladio adopts Vitruvius's view that the three vital issues in architecture are convenience, duration and beauty. Thus, here is an indication straightaway that the *Books* are concerned at least as much with the practical know-how of building construction as with aesthetics. "Beauty", says Palladio, "will result from the form and correspondence of the whole with respect to the several parts, of the parts with regard to each other, and of

4. When Giacomo Leoni's translation was first published in England in 1726, it was called (like Vitruvius' work) *Ten Books on Architecture*.

these again to the whole." After many pages of practical advice about building materials, foundations and walls, he deals in painstaking detail with the five Roman Orders (Tuscan, Doric, Ionic, Corinthian and Composite) as regards the proper ratios to be used (of column heights to widths and of intercolumniations and pilasters), the design of capitals and the swelling and diminution of columns. In a chapter on loggias, entries, halls and rooms he asserts that the proportions for rooms which succeed best are: a circle; a square; a square extended by the length of its diagonal; a square plus a third; a square plus a half; a square plus two-thirds; two squares. There is guidance on ceiling heights, doors and windows, chimneys, stairs and roofs.

5. *Villa Godi (Andrea Palladio, 1537).*

Book II includes drawings of town houses and villas of his own design (either projected or built) which were to be so influential and treated with something approaching religious fervour in later times. The best known, perhaps, are the Villas Godi, Chiericati, Pojana, Valmarana, Almerico Capra (La Rotunda), Barbaro, Pisani (at Bagnolo), Cornaro and Emo. However, as Inigo Jones and many other students of Palladio's work have demonstrated, the drawings in *I Quattro Libri* and the actual buildings seldom correspond. There are probably two main reasons for this. The first is that the client had died or run out of money before the full scheme could be implemented. In particular, many villas were designed with wings – normally containing farm buildings; rarely comprising service wings, the form in which they were to be taken up in the 18th century – and these were not always built as planned. The second reason is that writing, as he was, a practical building textbook, Palladio sometimes 'corrected' a design to show it as he would like it to be. It is not always easy to say whether this was a case of having second, improved, thoughts or whether something had prevented him from building in this way at the time.

6. Villa Cornaro (Andrea Palladio, 1553)

Book III deals with roads and bridges (including a design for 'a stone bridge of my own invention', of which more later), piazzas and basilicas and Book IV is concerned entirely with 'temples'. Here, as elsewhere in the *Four Books,* Palladio expresses what seems to be a deep and sincere belief in one true God but nowhere does he speak of Christ or of Christian beliefs or rituals. He describes different Roman temples as a guide to church design but does not question their suitability or relevance to Christian worship. (All this would, of course, be anathema to the likes of A.W.N.Pugin who did more than anyone to promote Gothic Revivalism in 19th-century Britain. "Men must learn", said Pugin, "that art ceased when it is said to have revived.")

It would be wrong to think of Palladio either as being influenced solely by Vitruvius or as the sole transmitter of Vitruvian notions. He became part of a sort of Humanist brotherhood in Vicenza headed by Giangiorgio Trissino, the name 'Palladio' being a 'humanist' name given to him as a reference to the wisdom of Pallas Athene. He would have been influenced not only by Trissino but by the architect Cornaro and the painter Falconelto. Above all he would have been inspired by the architect and painter Sebastiano Serlio whose *L'Architettura* has already been noted.

What impressed both his contemporaries and those who later went to Italy to study his work was the way he combined the ability to find the right practical solution with a masterly command of the idiom in which he worked. His buildings are often very simple giving them a timeless quality. Yet they are very varied – sometimes plain, sometimes elaborate; some convey strength, some lightness. He was a great architect because he

7. *Villa Barbaro (Andrea Palladio, 1557)*

produced many fine and interesting buildings which have stood the test of time, not because he invented a new style of architecture called Palladianism. It is easy enough to find instances of his own buildings not following his own design guidance or of oddities in his buildings.[5] All this is worth bearing in mind when judging the sometimes arid issue of whether a particular building should be called Palladian or something else.

We shall be leaving Palladio for a while waiting in the wings while we look at some of the more general characteristics of 'classicism', but there is one more name to mention before we do – that of Vincenzo Scamozzi (1552-1616). He is notorious for spending much of his time maligning Palladio (and publicising his own abilities) but you would not guess this from his work: he collaborated with Palladio on a number of projects and completed several of Palladio's works after his death, notably the Villa Rotunda. He produced an impressive body of architectural work in the tradition of Serlio and Palladio (including the sublime Villa Rocca Pisani) and a book (*Idea Dell'Architettura Universale*) that went beyond *I Quattro Libri*, at any rate in terms of length and the quality of the illustrations. He was self-assured to the point of arrogance and would be distressed to know that the style in which he worked is now known as 'Palladian'. In England he is perhaps best known for having exchanged a few words in Venice with Inigo Jones in 1613. Jones was not impressed by the meeting but came back with the book.

5. In the church of Il Redentore in Venice, for example, it is surprising to see the shafts of the interior columns divided horizontally between grey and off-white instead of being all one or the other, though this was part of a scheme whereby stone was used to a height that a man could reach with his hand and the rest was treated with a coat of special plaster. At least this was more expressive of the materials being used than in most of Palladio's buildings where it is often impossible to tell at a distance whether the surface consists of real stone or of a render imitating stone. In Palazzo Thiene, Vicenza, the rustic contains both.

3 The Nature of Classicism

All classical architecture, from the Renaissance onwards, is consciously and unashamedly derivative. The earliest practitioners were all seeking to re-create Roman architecture adapted to their own contemporary requirements. It was Palladio, in particular, who based many of his villas on traditional local forms while applying Roman orders and Roman details. Inigo Jones was to do the same sort of thing in England working out his own style in the process. With the Palladian Revival, it was now not only Palladio who was revered but Jones as well. Thus, early in the 18th century, a style of architecture developed which, as we shall see, was intended to be a new national architecture, patronised by the leading figures of the dominant political group (the Whig Party) and by prominent intellectuals, but which, in truth, was a product of a country, Italy, of which Whigs would, in other respects, be highly suspicious on account of its 'Popery'. Moreover, if this national style were to be maintained, all significant new buildings had to be seen by the self-appointed guardians of style as 'correct'. If there was a specific building design (whether executed or not) of Palladio or Jones on which a new building appeared to be based, it was more than half way to receiving the right nod. Even during the post-Palladian age, as Chambers, Adam, Wyatt, and others came to use an ever wider range of styles, there was rarely, if ever, a building designed *in vacuo*, so to speak, or out of pure imagination. (Perhaps Sir John Soane came nearest to it but was so piqued by a suggestion that he had invented a new order of architecture that he sued the perpetrator of such an insult – unsuccessfully as it happened.) There was always a point of origin, some relevant exemplar. Thus it is that the writings of architectural historians concerning the Georgian age are full of reference and allusion. There is probably nothing else quite like it in art criticism.[1]

Another characteristic of both Palladian and neo-classical architecture is that there is no attempt to 'express the structure' of a building as there is in gothic or modern architecture. It is the way a building appears as a piece of scenery in a street or in its rural setting that is paramount. Not only were structural forms hidden or disguised (by hiding a roof behind a parapet for example) but the architects would often deliberately falsify the structural attributes of a building, notably by giving the lowest 'rustic' floor a greater appearance of strength than it actually had: that is to say, it might look as if it consisted of solid blocks of masonry, while, in truth, it consisted of the same stone-faced rubble construction as the upper floors but channelled to give the effect of separate and massive blocks of stone. In Regency times, even a stone facing was often omitted in preference to stucco, applied and

1. The closest, perhaps, is in music, notably in relation to pop and R&B.

8. Austere classicism: Philipps House, Dinton (Jeffrey Wyatt, 1813-16)

painted to give the appearance of stone. Externally, the orders, when correctly used, gave a building the desired appearance of proportionality and refinement but were often merely 'applied' and had no structural function at all. And internally, timber and plaster became used more and more throughout the Georgian period to achieve the right visual effect. This was especially true of false Gothic vaulting, something which would disgust Pugin in years to come. We shall see how the search for the fashionably classical led to older timber-framed buildings being clad in brick or tiles.

Before this comes to sound like an attack on classicism let us turn to its great strengths. The first is its capacity for orderliness, whether in a single building or in a group of buildings. We saw in Chapter 2 that 'Order' was one of the necessary virtues emphasised by Vitruvius. He used that term in the sense of a reliance on the proper use of the 'orders' of architecture. His analysis of the five Roman orders (Tuscan, Doric, Ionic, Corinthian and Composite) was carried forward into the Renaissance and then into England by Inigo Jones and later throughout Britain by the Palladians. Each order sets the tone or style for a building and has its own set of rules about the design of columns, their bases and their entablature (the part of the building which the columns support, either actually or notionally). If the rules are followed, everything else drops into place. In the 18th century, this meant that orderliness could be achieved by a builder with limited design ability with the use of the many pattern books, or builders' guides, that came to be produced. This was the origin of the good manners and good taste the we expect to see in Georgian architecture.

All this prescription could give the impression that architects were denied creative freedom. In fact, the orders were only a start and the scope for variety was endless. The fact that there is no such thing as a single 'classical style' is the clearest demonstration of this. Classicism might mean anything from the simple purity of Bramante's Tempietto to the wild excesses of Bavarian Baroque or, in more local terms, from the austere simplicity of Philipps House, Dinton (fig.8) to the weirdly elaborate Rosewell House in Bath (fig.9); it embraces Mannerism, Baroque – in all its many manifestations – and Rococo as well as the more 'correct' Vitruvian forms encompassing Palladianism and 18th-century neo-classicism, including Greek Revival. Though, as we shall see more than once, these are only the most general of labels; each building is unique and to call it 'Palladian', say, or 'Baroque' is only to give some sort of pointer to its character.

9. *Fanciful classicism: Rosewell House, Bath (William Halfpenny, 1736)*

So an architect or experienced builder (or less experienced builder with a pattern book) had a wide range of options at his command. For example, an order did not need to be fully expressed. A column might be 'engaged' (with half or less of its circumference lost within a wall) or could be flattened to form a 'pilaster' where a column would not be appropriate. Or columns could be used in pairs or, when acting as a support, could be clustered in a quasi-sculptural fashion. Or they could be 'hidden', which is a way of saying omitted altogether, leaving just their entablature which could in turn be reduced or simplified, though leaving the proportions and rhythms unaffected. (A façade of a classical building without columns is denoted as 'astylar'.) A building could use more than one order, including, perhaps, a 'giant' order rising through two or more storeys, and the skill of the architect was needed to ensure that this was done successfully. The mood of a building can be affected by the spacing of the columns, the 'intercolumniation'. Vitruvius identified five types ranging from the equivalent of 1½ column diameters to 4 diameters (the most common is 'eustyle' at 2½ diameters).

Pediments could be designed in different ways with breaks, for example, either in the top or the base (both forms, confusingly, referred to as 'broken'). The rustication of walls, to give them the impression of blocks of masonry, could be carried out in many different ways. It might be confined to quoins and the surrounds of doors and windows; or used on the lower floor ('the rustic'), or on more than one floor or on the whole building. There were many different systems of jointing and of the treatment of the surface of the stone which could either be smooth or patterned in a variety of ways to resemble rock or, in the case of 'vermiculation', worm casts. There were different devices for breaking the skyline of a building (a favourite Palladian device) – acroteria on pediments or balls, urns or pine cones on parapets. Balustrades presented another whole range of design possibilities.

Doors, windows, porches, arches, domes, apses, niches all lent themselves to an almost infinite variety of treatments. Windows alone are the subject of immense variety, the so-called Venetian (or Serlian) window being a feature to which architects in Britain took a particular fancy and developed in imaginative ways (see page 204). On the grander estates there was much fun to be had with the design of gateways, lodges and bridges as well as all the make-believe temples, obelisks, caves, cottages and other adornments in the grounds.

Internally, even more opportunities for innovative design presented themselves. Apart from the disposition of the various rooms and internal spaces (we have seen the importance Palladio attached to their proportions), the designer of the building would normally be also responsible for the architectural features of the interior or, at the least, retain overall control of them – especially (in the case of a house) in the principal areas to be used by the family or to be seen by their guests. These could include staircases, balustrades, apses, niches, colonnades, chimney pieces, door and window surrounds (or even picture frames where the client attaches importance to the display of his pictures – as at Wilton House, for example), as well as the treatment of the floors or of the walls and ceilings (for which specialist plasterers might be brought in, working either to their own or the architect's design). The architect's involvement might even extend to the furniture (including the torchères), the door fittings and silverware for the table or sideboard. Both Robert Adam and James Wyatt excelled in this area which gave such scope for their design flair.

Another great strength of the classical age of building was the quality of its craftsmanship. Although the Industrial Revolution began late on in the

A range of classical details

10. *Clustered Doric columns and Doric entablature: The Council House, Bourne Hill, Salisbury (mid-18th century)*

11. *Ionic capital: Northgate House, Devizes (mid-18th century)*

12. *Corinthian pilasters and capitals: New Wardour Castle (James Paine, 1770-76)*

13. *Composite capitals: Amesbury Abbey (Thomas Hopper, 1834)*

14. *Scrolled pediment: No.5 St.Margaret's Street, Bradford-on-Avon (early 18th century)*

15. *Shell doorway hood: Marlborough House, Westbury (early 18th century)*

Georgian era, it did not lead to mass production of building materials until Victorian times. So all processes were undertaken by hand using methods and tools that had been gradually and painstakingly refined over many centuries. The skills of the medieval craftsmen were not set aside by classicism; they were merely harnessed to different ends. In his splendid book *Building the Georgian City*, James Ayres has shown how the building of a single house might involve all of the following skilful activities (which he fully describes):

> quarrying; masonry; stone carving; slate making; brick making; mortar making; bricklaying; timber extraction; carpentry; joinery; wood carving and wood turning; tool making; ironmongery; smithing; foundry working; plumbing (i.e. working in lead); glass making; glazing; plastering; painting (including the twin activity of paint making); wallpaper making.

(The Building of Bath Museum, at The Vineyards, Bath, tells, through a series of displays, the story of how the Georgian houses of Bath were designed, built, decorated and lived in.)

It would be wrong to imagine that work was always perfect, but, in general, standards were very high and jealously maintained through, for example, a system of lengthy apprenticeships. All this is just as well because most classical buildings rely on accuracy, precision and refinement to achieve the desired effect. This is why it is that the pleasing appearance of a building can be so easily destroyed not only by tasteless alterations but by poor craftsmanship – clumsy re-pointing of brickwork being a prime example. In other words, the production of fine buildings in a classical style would simply not have been achievable without high standards of craftsmanship. And this dependence on skilled people explains, first, why a huge number of Georgian buildings were put up by experienced craftsmen relying on pattern books for the design details and, second, why so many men who were designated as architects had come from a crafts background.

One other curious characteristic of classical architecture, of the 18th century in particular, which ought to be mentioned here is the almost total suppression (even in its churches) of any outward sign of the Christian religion to which the age paid lip service. The proverbial visitor from Mars would be convinced that the same pantheon of deities were still being worshipped as on its last trip to Earth during the days of Imperial Rome. Painting, sculpture and literature would all seem to confirm this impression. It would note that when British Earthlings died their memorials portrayed them in the dress of that previous age surrounded by the same nymphs and cherubs. What it might not understand was that the re-discovery of ancient wisdom had been accompanied by a casting off of what men saw as ignorance and superstition and was accompanied by a decline in religiosity.

There are two bizarre examples worth relating of the way the Georgian age was held in the thrall of Rome. In 1771, the Academician Benjamin West outraged his colleagues by painting the death of General Wolfe in contemporary costume (rather than in the style of Greece or Rome). This was regarded as an indignity to historical art and he had been called on to refrain not only by Sir Joshua Reynolds but by the Archbishop of Canterbury. He did not refrain and James Barry, in protest, painted the subject again with all the figures nude. Less than 60 years after these events, the railway age began and in 1830 William Huskisson, Member of Parliament for Chichester and later Liverpool, became the first person in England to be killed in a railway accident, at the opening of the Manchester and Liverpool line. In Chichester Cathedral, there is a memorial to him in the form of a life-size statue – in which he is dressed in a Roman toga.

An integral element of Roman art and literature was mythology, largely inherited from Greece. It therefore followed that Roman mythology seeped into the minds of every Georgian schoolboy as he struggled with his Latin texts. Few boys were schoolboys, of course – only the sons of the ruling élite. The myth we shall encounter more than once is that of Aeneas, the Trojan who wandered the Mediterranean world after the fall of Troy to create Ilium afresh. Whereas the Greeks, in Homer's *Odyssey*, delighted in the journeys of the man whose cleverness had led to Troy's downfall, the Romans celebrated the mythical story of Rome's founding, by Aeneas, as told in Virgil's *Aeneid*. Many Englishmen believed that the torch of Rome's greatness had been passed to their own country and that, in particular, the founder of the English nation was Brutus, not the conspirator of the 1st century BC, but the supposed great-grandson of Aeneas and first senator of Rome. It therefore followed that all the early English kings were descended from Brutus. Well, that's what many believed – with some interesting consequences.

4 England – The First Hundred Years

Classicism as an architectural style was to prevail in Britain for about 300 years – from about 1530; throughout most of the 18th century it was the only 'true' style and it remained the predominant one until about 1830 when the national imagination became fired by the Gothic Revival. Yet the influence of classicism was slow to reach these shores, partly on account of their remoteness from Northern Italy, the spiritual centre of the Renaissance, but principally on account of the drastic effects of Henry VIII's divorce from Catherine of Aragon, resulting in a break from the Church of Rome and a defensive military posture for many years towards mainland Europe. Whatever the reasons, the age of classical architecture in Britain began about 100 years after the start of the Italian Renaissance. That is not to say that what was happening in Italy in the early Quattrocento was what reached Britain 100 years later; that took another 100 years. In other words, what was being built in Britain (and, in this context, we really need to say England) during all that time (say, 1530-1630) only superficially resembled the buildings of the Quattrocento let alone the Cinquecento. It is interesting to compare the buildings of Italy and England at equivalent periods. Two of Wiltshire's most important medieval manor houses are at Great Chalfield and South Wraxall, both just north of Bradford-on-Avon. Both were begun in the 15th century after Brunelleschi had completed the Foundling Hospital in Florence (1421-24). This was about the time when St.Thomas's Church in Salisbury was being rebuilt – in the Perpendicular Gothic style – and churches would continue to be built in this style for another hundred years. Indeed, work would not start on the rebuilding of Bath Abbey until 1499. By then, Alberti had died and *De Re Aedificatoria* had been published. Work would start on Bramante's Tempietto in 1503 and on St.Peter's in Rome in 1506. By the time the first classical details were appearing in English buildings during, say, 1530-1540, Giulio Romano and Michelangelo were in their prime and pushing out the bounds of classicism, and Andrea Palladio had begun his distinguished career. Italy's great age of architectural discovery was virtually over; Britain's had hardly begun.

Renaissance ideas were not, of course, entirely unknown in the England of Henry VIII. Indeed, they were an important factor in the English Reformation and contributed to the dissatisfaction with the medieval institutions of the Church long before they were swept away. But, in the field of design, there was nothing that could be called classical architecture. There were only bits and pieces: the tomb that Henry had made for his father in Westminster Abbey by the Italian artist Pietro Torrigiano (1512),[1] a few of the details at Henry's extensions (from 1531) to Hampton Court (which was otherwise built in Tudor Gothic) and the choir stalls at King's College Chapel

1. Also attributed to Torrigiano is the exquisite Salisbury Chantry in Christchurch Priory, Dorset.

Cambridge (c.1532-1536). Nonsuch Palace, that glorious monstrosity begun in 1538, now marked only by a few mounds of earth and bricks near the Ewell by-pass, displayed all the latest samples of Renaissance design that Henry had seen at the Field of the Cloth of Gold and had heard about from descriptions of the court of his great rival, Francis I of France. Craftsmen were brought in from France, from the Low Countries and even, perhaps, from Italy to carry out the decorative work, which was a wonder to behold, but the structure was built by Englishmen in an English style. As Summerson puts it so neatly, "Classical architecture made its way in England not as a method of building but as a mode of decorative design." That could be the text for the whole of this chapter.

16. Detail of Lord Stourton's tomb, Stourton (1536)

The first glimpse of the new style to be found in Wiltshire is at St.Peter's, Stourton (on the National Trust's Stourhead estate) where the tomb of Edward, Lord Stourton, who died in 1536, contains a curious mix of Gothic and Renaissance forms. The sides of the tomb (fig.16) abound with tall arches and finials richly decorated in a style that would first have been in vogue about 200 years earlier. But it is framed by strips containing carvings of fluted vases and the corners consist of plain vertical strips (which Pevsner calls 'pilasters'). A precocious example of work with a classical flavour can be found at Lacock Abbey. William Sharrington acquired the Abbey in 1540

17. *Fire surround, Lacock Abbey (1540s).* *(© Crown copyright, N.M.R.)*

and undertook work to it over the following nine years showing a knowledge of classical forms in advance of the times (fig.17). But again, as far as Sharrington's Tower is concerned, for example, it is only the details, not the structure, that can be called classical. The famous octagonal stone table in the Tower could be taken as a foretaste of the equally famous and vigorous, yet unmistakeably Elizabethan, 'sea-dog' table at Hardwick and yet, like Lacock Abbey itself, the Gothic spirit seems somehow to linger within it. Another item from the middle of the 16th century that has survived is the so-called Holbein Porch, once a formal entrance to the north range of Wilton House from its court-yard but later rebuilt in what is now the private garden there. Its designer was certainly not the artist Hans Holbein, because he had died before it was built, but whoever it was demonstrated "an unusual understanding for the proportions and relationships of its superimposed Orders".[2] And, for all that has happened to it since, it must not be forgotten that Wilton House itself would have been a grand example of an early Tudor mansion when it was first built. The Tudor structure, of four wings around a courtyard, remains the framework for all that has followed and the east front retains some of its original character.

Under Henry VIII, church patronage of new building virtually ceased but Royal patronage was considerable. Elizabeth I made it her policy not to commit the same extravagances as her father. She hated Nonsuch, rarely using it, and built no new palace of her own. But she was quite content that her courtiers and ministers should overstretch themselves to build great houses in which she could be entertained. Thus began the age of the annual Royal Progress and the era of the Elizabethan prodigy house. Burghley House, Stamford, Lincolnshire (from 1575), Wollaton Hall, Nottinghamshire (1580-88), Hardwick Hall, Derbyshire (1590-97) and Montacute House, Somerset (1599) are some of the best known surviving examples of houses built with more than half an eye on the need to accommodate and entertain

2. See *Wilton House and English Palladianism* (RCHM).

18. Longleat House – "a work of art, noble, delicate and intelligent" (Sir John Thynne and Robert Smythson, 1572)

the Queen (and how bitter it must have been to Bess of Hardwick that the Queen never came to Hardwick Hall). But one of the most important of them all was Longleat, near Warminster (fig.18) built by the friend and near neighbour of Sharrington, Sir John Thynne. As a young man, Thynne had been taken into the household of Edward Seymour, later to become Lord Protector of the Boy King, Edward VI, during the early part of his reign. Thynne became his steward and this enabled him not only to build up a personal fortune but to acquire experience in a great building project, the original Somerset House in London, possibly the first complete building of the Renaissance in England. He managed to survive both Seymour's later disgrace (and execution) and the reign of Mary Tudor. Indeed, it was in the year of her marriage (1554) that he began work on his own estate at Longleat.

The history of the house is very complicated – Mark Girouard[3] identifies three Longleats by Thynne before 1572 – and at one stage there was a devastating fire. But the façade we see today was begun in 1572 and was, in effect, wrapped around what remained from earlier phases. The name 'Longleat' today is associated with lions, labyrinths and family fun and is overshadowed by the personality of Alexander Thynn,[4] the present (7th) Marquis of Bath and the commanding, albeit departed, presence of Henry Thynne, the 6th Marquis, who first turned Longleat into the important leisure venue that it is today. It is all too easy to fail to give the house itself the attention it deserves. For what Sir John Thynne eventually created was the

3. In *Robert Smythson and The Elizabethan Country House.*
4. This is the spelling he prefers to use.

most sublime and sophisticated of all the prodigy houses. As Girouard puts it: "It is perhaps the first Elizabethan house to have more than the charm of naivity or freshness. It is a work of art, noble, delicate and intelligent". Summerson calls it "the first great monument of Elizabethan architecture and perhaps, indeed, its greatest". Making the comparison once again with Italy, Palladio had died in 1580 so all his great villas had been built and *I Quattro Libri* published. But this only demonstrates that England was lagging behind in terms of correctly interpreting Roman architecture, something which was of no particular concern to those Elizabethans who were anxious to create fine buildings. Longleat is a demonstration that English architecture had followed a very different route from Italy and that a style had evolved which, at its best, could give rise to equally great examples of human imagination and creativity. But there was one vital difference. The legacy of Palladio was an approach to architecture that would prove a sound basis for what was to come; the English adventure had turned into a cul-de-sac from which it would find itself rescued only by an adoption of Palladian principles.

But this lies in the future. For the moment, to whom must we give credit for the design of Longleat? This presents difficulties for we are in an era in which to ask "who is the architect?" would have no meaning. The prime influence on the overall appearance of a house might come from the owner himself, from a friend who fancied his skill in that field or from one or more of the masons or other craftsmen employed on the particular job. At Lacock, for instance, we know that Sharrington employed a skilled mason, John Chapman (who also worked for Thynne), but almost certainly had a close involvement in the work himself. Now Thynne was not merely experienced in building but was one of a pioneering group (including Sharrington) that saw themselves as carrying the 'new' style into the Elizabethan age. At Longleat, it is likely that Thynne himself was the designer initially but that by the time Longleat House No.3 was being built he was placing more reliance on his two principal masons. These were Robert Smythson, whose name would be associated with many other houses, including Wollaton Hall and Hardwick Hall, and a Frenchman, Allen Maynard, who had been involved at earlier stages and who is also known to have carved at least some of the chimney pieces.

When Thynne's neighbour Sir Matthew Arundell refitted his castle at Wardour (the one we now call 'Old Wardour') in 1578 he employed Robert Smythson; so it is no surprise that the details are reminiscent of those at Longleat (fig.19). A more extensive example of an Elizabethan house (though only the porch and adjacent bays have survived later re-modelling) is Corsham Court begun in 1582. (This is a house to which we will return more than once because the architectural history is so complex that it would fill a book; as indeed it does – *Architects at Corsham Court* by Frederick J.Ladd.) A much more unusual house of the period was Longford Castle, at Britford, near Salisbury, completed in 1591. This was the seat of Sir Thomas Gorges who married Helena, the Swedish widow of the Marquis of Northampton who had been Queen Elizabeth's Maid of Honour. She is also said to have been instrumental in securing the gift by the Queen to her husband of the valuable contents of a Spanish galleon after the Armada. This enabled him to complete his house, which is in a form not seen before in England, namely triangular[5] with a turret in each corner. But what concerns us here is the loggia (considerably altered in the 19th century) that ran between two of the towers. Not only was it a two-storey loggia – the first in England – but was the first example in England of Flemish Mannerism, with pedimented gables, blocked pilasters and caryatids. This is a foretaste of the Jacobean age to which we must now proceed.

***19**. An example of Sir Matthew Arundell's and Robert Smythson's work at Old Wardour Castle (1578)*

There may not have been any undue concern at this time to reproduce either the spirit or the correct details of the ancient Romans, but there was certainly an eagerness to break with the past, to be new and excitingly different. The inspiration for the earliest essays at classicism came from a

5. Gorges moved in the same circles as the poet Edmund Spenser and was possibly influenced by the description of the Castle of Temperance in Book 2 of the *Faerie Queene* – "The frame thereof was partly circular / And part triangular – O work divine".

variety of sources – travellers' recollections of what they had seen (more in France and the Low Countries than across the Alps), the knowledge and experience of craftsmen who had come here from countries where Renaissance forms were longer established and, perhaps the source that became the most important, books produced by experienced builders. In the Georgian era, such books, by then referred to as 'pattern books', proved, on the whole, to have a valuable influence, but in the Elizabethan and Jacobean age they were a mixed blessing. Now, it is true that, as early as 1550, the Duke of Northumberland had actually sent one of his household to Italy to study the buildings, both ancient and modern. This was John Shute (d.1563) who went on to produce a book, *The First and Chief Groundes of Architecture*, published in the year he died. It included illustrations of the five Roman orders, based on Serlio. Serlio's books were themselves available in England at this time as were Vitruvius' *Ten Books*. But you would not have thought so from the results. The idea of symmetry had been grasped early on, at Somerset House, but the proper use of the orders was not yet understood. A few like Thynne and Smythson had worked out their own system for producing a harmonious façade without over-ornamention. But by the time James I had come to the throne, builders were looking for pattern books with designs that fulfilled the expectations of their employers for greater novelty. The ones that proved the most popular were those (mostly Flemish) that showed elaborately ornamental schemes with large areas of 'strapwork' (the best known of these books being by Hans Vredeman de Vries from Amsterdam). Strapwork, deriving its name from the similarity of its appearance to strips of cut leather, had been a popular feature (especially on gables) of buildings in the Netherlands from about 1540. There is some strapwork on the wall parapets and on the façade of Longleat but it is barely noticeable (fig.20). The depths of late Elizabethan and Jacobean taste had not yet been plumbed. It is, perhaps, significant that far more conspicuous are the displays of strapwork on an unfortunate gable addition to Brunel's Bath Spa railway station and on C.E.Davis's much-maligned Empire Hotel, also in Bath.

20. *Longleat House, detail*

21. *South Wraxall Manor, fireplace (c.1598).*
(© Crown copyright, N.M.R.)

Perhaps the finest display in Wiltshire of English Renaissance exuberance is in two of the fireplaces at South Wraxall Manor, one of them, though not the one illustrated (fig.21), bearing the date 1598. Those at Stockton House, Stockton are in similar style.

Two notable examples of Jacobean houses in Wiltshire are Charlton Park, near Malmesbury, (1607) and The Hall, Bradford-on-Avon (1610). The latter's impressive fenestration brings to mind the jingle about Derbyshire's Hardwick Hall, where there was 'more glass than wall'. Neither, in fact, are examples of unduly exuberant Jacobean architecture; it is even possible that Robert Smythson produced a sketch design for The Hall for a local man to follow. A rare and interesting example of a smaller town house, probably Jacobean (though with earlier origins), can be found in Salisbury, namely No.17 The Close. The doorway, in Jacobean style, is a Victorian addition but its whimsical decoration is inconsistent with the strong simple lines of its windows and the pilaster-like buttresses on each side of the front face.

Meanwhile, Wiltshire's churches were filling up with the distinctive classical memorials of the Elizabethan and Jacobean era, bursting with columns, arches and kneeling or recumbent figures, and it is here that picking and mixing from the pattern books is more likely to be in evidence. There are fine examples to be found at Lydiard Tregoze, Westbury, Chippenham, Broad Hinton and in Salisbury Cathedral. Bath Abbey has a few, fighting for attention amongst all those memorials from the 18th and 19th centuries. This style of memorial would have been scorned, a century later, by the Palladians but we enjoy them today for their touching charm and their vigour, though the Hertford tomb (1621) in Salisbury Cathedral with its towering, pretentious bulk (almost totally covering one of the cathedral's high windows) offers little delight to the eye. After this, the Gorges memorial to the north (to Sir Thomas and his Swedish wife), from 1635, is like a breath of fresh air – though its curious open design is one all on its own and fits no particular style.

So classicism in England had got off to a patchy start in Tudor times, had reached exciting heights in some of the Elizabethan prodigy houses but, by the early 17th century, was beginning to deteriorate into a style that might have given the rest of Europe an impression of England's cultural backwardness were it not for the great respect in which her writers and poets were held at that time. But then appeared Inigo Jones.

5 Inigo Jones

Architecture undergoes constant reappraisal; the reputation of an architect may suffer as a result of the different tastes of later generations only to be reinstated as the tides of taste ebb and flow. Yet the eminence of Inigo Jones (1573-1652) amongst British architects has never faltered.[1] Not only was he the first Briton to show a proper understanding of the architecture of the Italian Renaissance but he produced a range of work himself that would have its own influence on those that followed him. So great has been his reputation that, during the 18th and 19th centuries, false attributions to him abounded; where any building faintly resembled his known work, in the absence of any inconvenient evidence to the contrary, it was readily embraced by the proud owner or the local community as 'the work of Inigo Jones'. (This could be called 'the Inigo Jones Popular Tendency'.) During the 20th century, as architectural historians lost confidence in local tradition, they became too quick to minimise Jones's involvement, even where the quality of the building itself made another hand unlikely ('the Inigo Jones Architectural Historian Tendency'). One such building was the south front of Wilton House. Another was that great landmark of English building design, Coleshill House, Berkshire. But the tide has now turned in Jones's favour and, if these two works can be safely restored to him, the scale of his lasting achievement becomes truly immense.

22. *Plaster bust of Inigo Jones, Trafalgar House, Standlynch: his influence on classicism in Britain was immense*

He was very much a creature of the court, having been engaged, first by James I and then by Charles I, as a painter and designer of stage sets, especially those for court masques, and he continued in that capacity even after his status as the court architect was firmly established. Yet his last years were spent during the period of the Interregnum, and, though deprived of Royal patronage and by now in his seventies, he continued to produce work of lasting significance. Little is known of his early life, though it is

1. Even John Ruskin, for all his detestation of Renaissance art, regarded Inigo Jones as a man 'of real intellect and imagination' (*The Stones of Venice*, Chapter 1, XXXVIII).

23. *Queen's House, Greenwich (Inigo Jones begun 1616) – like an alien visitation.* (*© Crown copyright, N.M.R.*)

certain that he went to Italy at an early age, perhaps spending several years there, learning to draw in the fluid Italian manner and absorbing Italian architecture. In 1613, he was granted the 'reversion' of the post of Surveyor to the King's Works, the greatest post in building, and the same year set off with Thomas Howard, 2nd Earl of Arundel, to Italy where he certainly visited Vicenza, making notes in the margins of his own copy of *I Quattro Libri*, and met Scamozzi who had been a pupil of Palladio and whose book *Idea dell'Architettura Universale* would later be another important influence on Jones. Most importantly, he learnt to reject the mannerism of the likes of Michelangelo and formed the belief that architecture – or, at least, 'outward ornament' – should be 'solid, proportionable according to rule, masculine and unaffected'.

His stage-set designs, though portraying buildings that were fantastical in a way that 'real' architecture could never quite be, opened his patrons' eyes to a world of sophisticated classicism of a kind they had not seen before. And when, in 1616, work began on the Queen's House at Greenwich (fig.23), its simple unaffected lines must have seemed like something from another planet. Its design predates by five years, for example, the 'Old House' in Hereford's Market Place, a quaint relic of 'Olde England' with its high triple gables and elaborate timber framing (fig.24). As the King's architect, which he had become in 1615, nearly all the buildings he designed were in London. We have seen how, through the Inigo Jones Popular Tendency, many buildings have been attributed to him. Bath's former Guildhall[2] is an example and the archway at Fonthill Bishop (fig.86, p.109) another. But there is only one building outside London that has survived to which his name can be linked with any confidence and that is Wilton House in Wiltshire.

It is fitting that this should be so because Jones had had a long association with the Earls of Pembroke and with Wilton House. William Herbert, the 3rd Earl, had certainly been an early patron of Jones in some form or another and may have paid for, or even accompanied him on his early visits to Italy. There are two recorded occasions during William's time on which Jones was required to attend Wilton – in 1615 to meet King James and in 1620 to investigate Stonehenge for His Majesty. After William's death in 1630, his brother Philip succeeded as 4th Earl and embarked on major work to the house and grounds, whilst retaining much of the Tudor house. According to the Wiltshire antiquarian and man of letters, John Aubrey, the use of Inigo Jones as architect had been personally recommended by Charles I. (Jones would almost certainly have been Philip's first choice anyway, but the King's words would have amounted to an approval to employ the King's Surveyor.) But, according to Aubrey, Jones was too busy elsewhere (at Greenwich) and suggested that his assistant Isaac de Caus, who had already been responsible for laying out the new gardens, should be appointed. Now, on account of

24. *The 'Old House', Hereford (1621) – a relic of Olde England*

2 In *An Essay Towards a Description of Bath*, John Wood gives quite a plausible explanation for the attribution to Inigo Jones: Jones's mother (Wood had been told) was the daughter of a Bath Master Clothier and he was a "near relation" to the mother of George Trim, the founder of Trim Street; he was prevailed upon to provide a design for the Guildhall while he was in Bath to examine the bathing cisterns; the style of the Ionic capitals was of a pre-Scamozzi design ("where the Rind of the Volute runs strait along the Face of the Capital") that accords with ancient Roman precedents that, Wood says, only Jones would have been familiar with at the time.

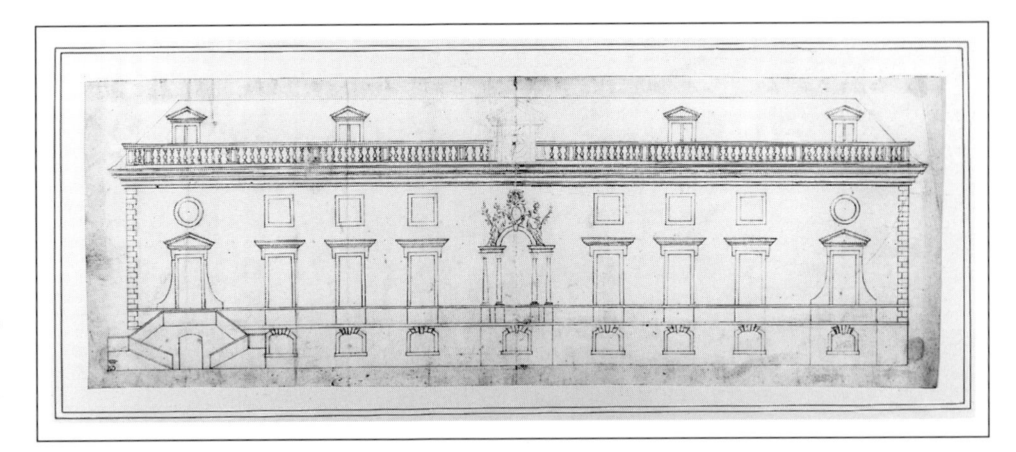

25. *Wilton House: the reduced scheme. (British Architectural Library, R.I.B.A., London)*

this reference to de Caus, and the fact that his name appears on certain drawings, his involvement at Wilton has been elevated, through the working of the Inigo Jones Architectural Historian Tendency, to that of architect. But it has always seemed strange that an expert in garden layouts and waterworks should be responsible for such a sophisticated and influential design – especially when it is compared with a building he is *known* to have designed at Wilton, the rather clumsy and old-fashioned stables that can be seen distantly on the hillside to the south-west of the house. But apart from the fact that Aubrey himself refers to the work being done "not without the advice and approbation of Mr.Jones", current scholarship has revived the more plausible authorship of the work as that of Inigo Jones and subordinated de Caus's role to that of a clerk of works.[3] When a disastrous fire in 1647 led to a second rebuilding, there is no evidence that de Caus was involved at all. The only name to appear on any of the exterior drawings was John Webb, by that time Jones's pupil and assistant. However, there are some notes in Jones's handwriting on many of the interior drawings and it is widely assumed that the hand of Jones lies behind what can now be seen at Wilton including the south front (facing the River Nadder) and the famous Single and Double Cube Rooms. It was the Double Cube Room that was virtually designed around the Earl's paintings by Van Dyck. Van Dyck was the King's painter and no other subject had amassed such a large collection of his work. This, coupled with the use of the King's architect, is an indication that Wilton House must have enjoyed greater prestige than any other great house at that time. Certainly, John Aubrey tells us, Charles "did love Wilton above all other places".

Philip, the 4th Earl, had originally intended to extend his house so that it would take on palace-like proportions stretching across the whole width of de Caus's formal gardens. The original elevations for the house show such a building with a central pediment and the Venetian window (now the

3. See especially *Architecture Without Kings* by Timothy Mowl and Brian Earnshaw and an article by the same authors, 'Inigo Jones Restored', in *Country Life*, 31st January 1992.

26. *The South Front, Wilton House (Inigo Jones, begun 1647). (Wilton House Trust)*

central feature of the design) being repeated on the other side. At that stage the distinctive end towers were not a feature of the design. Philip may have felt that not even his resources would stretch to the full scheme and so it was curtailed to its present size (figs.25 & 26). The one surviving Venetian window became the central feature and towers were added at each end to match the effect of the surviving Tudor towers as well as to give emphasis to the ends. The towers have been given false quoins to give the impression that they protrude from the front of the building whereas they are in fact merely a continuation of it in the same plane. This may be further confirmation that they are an added after-thought.

The central Venetian window (fig.27) is an example of what Wittkower[4] calls 'Pseudo-Palladianism'. The original tripartite form of the Venetian window was used as an integral part of the exterior of a building. The example often cited to illustrate this is Palladio's Basilica[5] at Vicenza (fig.28) where the typical Venetian window shape is used as an elegant device in the design of an arcade – in this case a two-storey loggia cleverly constructed around three existing medieval halls. Palladio had probably been influenced in this by Serlio and also by Sansovino's design, twelve years earlier, for the Library in Venice (the building which faces the Doge's Palace across the Piazzetta di San Marco). At any rate, thereafter, this satisfying shape was plucked out of its original context and used as a free-standing shape to form either a doorway or a window. It would be misleading to suggest that this

4. See his *Palladio and English Palladianism*.
5. More properly, the Loggia del Palazzo della Ragione.

27 (above, left). Venetian window, Wilton House. (Wilton House Trust)

28 (above, right). Palazzo della Ragione (Basilica), Vicenza (Andrea Palladio, 1546)

was solely a phenomenon of English Palladianism – though it was used there a great deal. Scamozzi's influential Villa Rocca Pisani (1576), for example, uses large and elegant Venetian windows on three of its sides (the fourth containing a porticoed entrance). Nevertheless, here at Wilton is an early English example of the free-standing Venetian window which was to be used again and again by the neo-Palladians as well as by countless housebuilders right through the Georgian era.

Superimposed on this window are two carved human figures and a cartouche containing the Pembroke coat of arms. Again, there is a touch of 'Pseudo-Palladianism' here. The use of two figures above an arch or window was a common device of the Cinquecento, either in the form of stone figures on the exterior of a building (see figs.29 and 30 for examples from the work of Palladio and of Scamozzi) or of painted figures over an internal doorway, forming part of a larger fresco. But in all cases the figures either repose on either side of a pediment or are used to fill the spandrel of an arch. Now,

Jones does indeed use pairs of figures in this orthodox fashion in the decoration of the Double Cube Room – above the doorway that leads to the Great Ante-Room (on either side of a triangular pediment broken at the top by a cartouche of the Pembroke arms) and in the over-mantel of the massive fire surround (on either side of a curly pediment, again topped by a cartouche). But here, on Wilton's south façade, the figures and the cartouche are used to form an upward extension of the shape of the window to the cornice of the outside wall in a way that is both exuberant and richly satisfying. Yet, curiously, the use of human figures in this way is not something that was taken up by the neo-Palladians, at any rate on exteriors. Did they feel that they ought not try to compete with this coup that had been pulled off with such panache, or did they feel that it was all too bizarre and frivolous for the serious endeavours on which they were engaged?

29 *(above, left). Reclining figures: Palazzo Valmarana, Vicenza (Andrea Palladio, 1565)*

30 *(above, right). Reclining figures: loggia, Palazzo Trissino, Vicenza (Vincenzo Scamozzi, c.1576)*

The Double Cube Room, and the other State Rooms at Wilton, represent another side of Jones's character and genius. His remarks quoted earlier, which come from his sketch book for the year he succeeded to the Surveyorship, need to be given their proper context:

> For as outwardly every wise man carries himself gravely in public places, yet inwardly has imagination and fire which sometimes flies out unrestrained, just as Nature flies out to delight or amuse us, to move us to laughter, contemplation, or even horror; so in architecture the outward ornament is to be solid, proportionable according to rule, masculine and unaffected.

31. The Double Cube Room, Wilton House. (© Crown copyright, N.M.R.)

Certainly the Double Cube Room has more to do with delight and amusement than it has with gravity (fig.31). Except for its 'double cube' proportions and the careful, if elaborate, design of the door surrounds, there is little about it that we would associate with Palladianism. (Pevsner suggests that it was "stimulated by the semi-classical, semi-Baroque decoration of France".) But this may be to confuse what we have come to regard as Palladianism with the actual works of Palladio. In his Palazzo Barbarano in Vicenza there are rooms very reminiscent of the State Rooms of Wilton House. They do not share their large size or soaring grandeur but the elaborate friezes, the clusters of fruit, the little consoles on top of the cornice, the way the walls curve into the ceiling, even the decorative faces that look out from the plasterwork are all so similar to the equivalent features at Wilton House that it is unlikely that Inigo Jones had not seen these rooms and not been influenced by them.[6] Sir William Chambers would later be critical of some of its design features – the coving is too deep, the internal arch of the Venetian window cuts off the entablatures and "rises into the cove very disagreeably" and he thought the fruit in the heavy garlands that decorate the walls looked like bunches of turnips.

6. On the other hand, there is no precedent in Palladio's work for the rich and elaborate doorway surrounds at Wilton.

All of this really goes to show that Inigo Jones was very much his own man. His attention to detail and his analysis of historical precedents were painstaking but his designs were his own and, as an architect, he never lost the flair and imagination that had set him apart as a stage designer. And more was to come. The style of house architecture that was developed during the Interregnum was different both from the style we call 'Jacobean' and from Jonesian Palladianism. The dilemma for the leading men of the brave new world of the Commonwealth was that, although, under the influence of Inigo Jones, the earlier Jacobean style had been discredited, all his previous work had been for Royalty or royal supporters and could no longer be regarded as politically correct. So a style was developed that took the essence of the new classicism that Jones had introduced but in an idiom that was spare in its details and virtually lacking in outward ornamentation – no columns, no pilasters, no temple fronts. Mowl and Earnshaw call it Puritan Minimalism. They also suggest that it was developed by no less than Inigo Jones; that so far from going into ignominious retirement after he was captured at Basing House he continued to live in comfortable apartments and went on working for anyone who wished to use his immense talents. (It must not be forgotten that the last rebuilding of Wilton's south front and State Rooms was as late as 1647.) An early (and glorious) example of the Puritan Minimalist House was Coleshill House, Berkshire, tragically burnt down in 1952 and the ruins demolished. Built in 1649-50, the design of the house had been traditionally attributed to Jones but, through the workings of the Inigo Jones Architectural Historian Tendency, he was stripped of its primary authorship early in the 20th century in favour of Roger Pratt who was a relative of the man for whom it was built, was certainly involved in its execution and would go on to build a number of houses in a similar style (including Kingston Lacy in Dorset). But at the time of Coleshill he had barely begun his own career and to produce a design of such refinement so early on is most unlikely. There should be nothing surprising about Jones's authorship in the light of his professed preference for outward architecture that was "solid, proportionable ... masculine and unaffected". At any rate, it was a style that would survive the Restoration though rooted in the Commonwealth.

But there is one piece of Palladianism with which the present chapter should close. Whereas Inigo Jones would continue to innovate, his pupil John Webb (1611-1672), though not untalented, lacked his originality and would continue to follow Palladian precedents. He was a Somerset man and a relative by marriage of Jones; he would soon be at work again in Wiltshire, this time for the Duke of Somerset at Amesbury Abbey about eight miles to the north of Wilton. Whereas the town of Wilton lies between the Nadder and the Wylye (which join close to Wilton House), Amesbury lies on the River Avon, the largest of Salisbury's five rivers. And whereas the Abbey at Wilton had been granted at the Dissolution to William Herbert (later the first Earl of Pembroke), Amesbury's ancient Abbey had been granted to another great

32. *Gate pillars, Amesbury Abbey (John Webb, 1661)*

man of State, Edward Seymour, soon to become Duke of Somerset and Lord Protector at the beginning of the short reign of his nephew, Edward VI. All that remain of the house he built there are two unusual Tudor Gatehouses, Kent House and Diana House, which can both easily be seen from the A345 between the 'Countess' roundabout on the A303 and the centre of Amesbury. For in 1661, the house itself was rebuilt by the 2nd Duke of Somerset (of a later creation). Despite the date, this is another example of a long-standing mis-attribution to Inigo Jones. It is only in recent times that the architect has been confirmed as John Webb though its Palladian credentials are so powerful that it would have been easy to accept that it was by the hand of the great master himself. Indeed, it was only in the 20th century that the work of Webb was untangled from that of his master and the influence of his own work on that of Burlington and his entourage acknowledged. Sadly, Webb's house too has virtually disappeared (though more will be said about it when the later work is considered in Chapter 16) and only a pair of striking and elegant gate pillars[7] remain (fig.32). And that marks the end of true Palladianism in our area. The Palladian Revival would not take place for another 60 years or so. Part of one country house, the traces of another and a pair of gateposts may not sound an impressive collection of Palladian survivals from the era of Inigo Jones but few counties of England can boast any at all.

7. They bear a striking resemblance to the pair of gate posts (illustrated in *Vitruvius Britannicus*) that once stood to the east of Wilton House (when the road from Salisbury still ran up to the gates and close to the house).

6 Before the Palladian Revival

The period between the death of Inigo Jones and the Palladian Revival, roughly 1660 to 1720, produced some of the most interesting, and certainly most varied, buildings of the classical era. The classical style was by now well established, builders and craftsmen were now fully conversant with the new idioms and, in the wake of Inigo Jones, there were more building practitioners who could be regarded as architects. On the other hand, there was an absence of any insistence on a 'correct' style, The high-minded censorship of the Palladians was yet to come. So the period produced architects as varied as Sir Roger Pratt, William Talman, Sir Christopher Wren, Nicholas Hawksmoor and Sir John Vanbrugh. It saw a final flowering of what Summerson has called Artisan Mannerism and the birth of English Baroque.

But this is not to say that the Palladian principles, first introduced by Jones, had been forgotten or ignored. It would be simplistic to suggest that Palladianism had died with Inigo Jones and was waiting to be brought back to life by the Palladian Revival. There was clearly no such discontinuity. Indeed, Worsley argues that Sir Roger Pratt (1620-1684) had not only absorbed the lessons to be learnt from Inigo Jones but was familiar with Palladio's villa designs in *I Quattro Libri* and adapted them to the English climate far more successfully than the so-called Palladian architects. Mowl and Earnshaw would go further, of course, and argue that the credit for such successful adaptation should go to Inigo Jones himself and that Pratt was merely following where Jones had led. Worsley also shows that the concerns of Campbell and Hawksmoor, for example, were very similar, and to suggest that there was a divide between a Baroque Group and a Palladian Group would be a misconception.

The period is well exemplified by the houses of Salisbury's Cathedral Close. Standing assertively in North Walk, facing straight down Bishop's Walk towards the Bishop's Palace, is No.19 The Close (fig.33) built for a lawyer, Francis Hill, in 1667. (The Palace is now a school and No.19 became a theological college in the 1870s and is now a diocesan educational centre.) This is a red-brick house with stone dressings in a classical form stripped down, in the English tradition of its time, to simple essentials (even the door hood is an 18th-century addition). It has two principal floors of equal height divided by a projecting band of stone and covered by a roof of medium pitch that overhangs all round. It has nine bays with the outer bays projecting on a 2:5:2 design. The roof is fully hipped at each end and contains five equally spaced dormer windows. The design has rhythm and symmetry with a hint of the Roman orders in the cornice below the roof but otherwise is devoid of Roman architectural details. In fact, it is a typical post-Restoration gentleman's house of the type first developed by Inigo Jones and continued

33. *No.19 The Close, Salisbury (c.1677)*

by Roger Pratt. No.9 The Close, on the corner of Bishop's Walk, was probably built about the same time as No.19 and shares many of its characteristics even if it faces the street in a rather more demure fashion. Its projecting brick quoins and plat band have been painted to give the impression of stone.

34. *Matron's College, The Close, Salisbury (1682)*

35. Mompesson House, The Close, Salisbury (1701)

Matrons' College, Nos.39-46 The Close (fig.34), was built a few years later (1682) but seems to give away its age more readily than Nos.9 and 19. This is partly due to the fact that it alone has retained its original mullioned windows. Also, its more ornate details give it enormous charm but somehow prevent the building from sharing the almost timeless quality of these other houses. Otherwise it shares many of their characteristics although, to break up the length of the building (which has a 2:13:2 rhythm), a pediment has been introduced above the three central bays. This contains a cartouche of the arms of Charles II topped by a cheerful crowned lion and flanked by large swags of fruit. The College was built for its founder, Bishop Seth Ward, by Thomas Glover of Harnham and it was probably designed by him as well, despite a long-standing attribution to Sir Christopher Wren. Surprisingly, the brickwork in all these three houses has been laid in English bond (with alternating courses of all headers and all stretchers) a system which had generally been replaced by Flemish bond by about 1640.

It is only as we reach Mompesson House, No.53 The Close (fig.35), that we experience a foretaste of Georgian elegance and sophistication – though this is a Queen Anne house, built in 1701 for Charles Mompesson MP. As in the two other houses and Matrons' College, the roof and dormers are still a prominent feature of the design though the roof itself now stops short of the vertical line of the wall. Its narrower windows give it a more tight-knit urban feel[1] but it is the use of ashlar stone facings and finely carved central details that sets it apart from what we have seen till now.

1. This enabled it to masquerade as the London house of Mrs.Jennings in the 1995 film *Sense and Sensibility*.

36. Myles Place, The Close, Salisbury (1718)

Perhaps it was the building of Mompesson House that inspired James Harris, in about 1705 to add a new ashlar-faced front wing to No.15 The Close, now called Malmesbury House (James Harris's great-grandson, the fourth in a line of Harrises to be called James, became the 1st Earl of Malmesbury in 1800). In about 1720, Arundells, No.59, was given a rebuilt front in a style very similar to No.15; both have deep roof overhangs and plain window openings set in an ashlared wall of masonry blocks of Chilmark stone so similar in size and shape that it is as if the same team of masons were employed at both sites.

The last house to be considered in The Close, Myles Place, No.68 (fig.36), comes towards the end of the period we are looking at. It was begun in 1718 – for another lawyer, William Swanton who had married the daughter of Francis Hill of No.19. The first obvious change from what has gone before is the apparent absence of a roof (only an aerial photograph reveals its peaks and troughs). There are four floors, two principal floors of equal height raised above a basement level, with discreet smaller windows, and surmounted by another tier of smaller windows. On its front façade, four giant pilasters rise through the principal floors and the doorway, reached by a flight of twelve stone steps, is flanked by fluted Corinthian pilasters and surmounted by a thin, segmental pediment containing a coat of arms. The windows have stone cills and prominent keystones. There are many more Roman details here. But can it be called Palladian? First of all, leaving aside what it actually looks like, its date alone makes it an unlikely example of the Palladian Revival. It would have to have been designed by a prominent Palladian architect and the designer of No.68 is not known. But it is the massive presentation of its façade that contradicts any Palladian influence. Most of the Palladian villas were quite small, or, at least, avoided any impression of bulk by having few storeys and a strong central feature. Windows were smaller and fewer. The original central portion of Stourhead House is a good example of an early Palladian design in this country (see fig.54, p.70). By contrast, Myles Place presents an overpowering, almost oppressive face to the world. The details may be consistent with being Palladian but the general style must be marked down as Baroque.

The use of the term 'Baroque' requires some explanation. The dictionary definition (taken from the *Concise Oxford Dictionary*) is "highly ornate and extravagant in style especially of European art, architecture and music of the 17th and 18th centuries". In architecture, the style was taken to extremes in the churches and palaces of Austria and southern Germany. Writing of such places in *Byways, Leaves from an Architect's Note-book* (1929), Sir Reginald Blomfield says "... in Baroque architecture there is always a hint of nightmare in the background, something vague and ill-defined and not quite wholesome ...". Well, this can hardly be said of Myles Place or of the other houses of the early 18th century that we shall soon be looking at and yet 'Baroque' (very often 'provincial Baroque') is the term generally applied to them. So what are we to make of this? In this context, i.e. English architecture of the early 18th century (including, perhaps, the last few years of the 17th century), it means no more than that the general design of the building is classical but remains untouched by the Palladian revival. And 'Palladian revival' needs to be narrowly construed as the outcome of the movement we shall be looking at in the next chapter, that of 'going back to basics' as far as the works of Palladio and Inigo Jones are concerned. A good sprinkling of classical features is not enough. You would normally expect to find a *piano nobile*, a limited amount of external decoration and a high proportion of wall to window.[2] But it is not clear cut and there is certainly room for different views as well as confusion. For example, Kingston Maurward House near Dorchester, Dorset (now used as an agricultural training college), was built at about the same time as Myles Place, in the same tall rectangular style, with the same bold giant pilasters and with an elaborate roofline. It is almost certainly the work of Thomas Archer, exclusively an architect of the English Baroque. Yet it is regularly described as Palladian.

2. This penchant for small windows (borrowed from Veneto with its summer heat) was a source of irritation (or amusement) to many at the time and, inevitably, it gave Sarah, Duchess of Marlborough, something else to complain about: "I observe one aversion (our present architects) have, which is light, and that is the reverse of my inclination. My Lord Herbert [later 9th Earl of Pembroke – see Chapter 9] particularly seems to dislike extremely windows in his room".

37. Urchfont Manor (c.1680)

Considering the long history of The Close, which was laid out early in the 13th century, it is remarkable that so many of its houses were either built or re-styled in this period of 1660 to 1720 (another is Myles Place's neighbour, The Walton Canonry (No.69), which may be by the same (unknown) architect). The character of The Close owes a great deal to this group of houses and is a good demonstration of how the Palladian style, to which Bath, for example, owes its particular form of classical refinement, should not be regarded as an essential prerequisite to good taste in the classical age.

Two fine mansions of the late 17th century in Wiltshire, showing many of the the same characteristics as Nos.9 and 19 The Close and Matrons' College, Salisbury are Ramsbury Manor and Urchfont Manor, both c.1680. Of the two, Urchfont (fig.37) is the more easily accessible, being used by Wiltshire County Council as an adult education centre. A rather grander example is the great house which the 6th Duke of Somerset built at Marlborough, from about 1699, and which now forms part of Marlborough College ('C1 House'). In similar style, but of a more modest size, are Dial House, West Lavington (1691) (fig.38), Moot House, Downton (c.1700) (fig.39), Gifford Hall, Broughton Gifford (c.1700) and Hyde's House, Dinton, re-faced early in the 18th century. An especially pleasing example of this style of early 18th-century house is Poulton House, just outside Marlborough (fig.40). It has much in common with Moot House but the greater width of its projecting centre, as well as its corresponding larger central pediment and greater overall height, give it a nobler presence.

38. *Dial House, West Lavington (1691)*

39. *Moot House, Downton (c.1700)*

40 *(above). Poulton House, Marlborough (1706). (Tim Mowl)*
41 *(below, left). No.53 Payne's Hill, Salisbury (late 17th century)*
42 *(below, right). The Vicarage, Church Street, Market Lavington (early 18th century)*

43. No.23 High Street, Cricklade (1708)

Fine urban examples are Kingsbury Hill House, Marlborough (c.1700), No.53 Payne's Hill, Salisbury (late 17th century) (fig.41), Trinity Hospital, Salisbury (1705) and Marlborough House, Westbury (early 18th-century). The Vicarage, Church Street, Market Lavington (fig.42) is an interesting example of a house with the same prominent roof as all the buildings above but with curved, Baroque window heads with prominent keystones that place it firmly in the 18th century. Nearby, in High Street, it is surprising to come across a brick building with stone mullions and quoins, 'The Red House', which is a former farm house; it has survived here from the 17th century and is reminiscent of No.9 The Close, Salisbury, though a good deal plainer and without any of its charm. The finest example in Wiltshire of 'Puritan Minimalism' – though a very late one – is a house at Cricklade, 23 High Street (fig.43). The year carved over the doorway is 1708 but the spirit of Coleshill lives on in this deceptively simple design.

Houses which, like Myles Place, have 'correct' Roman motifs but are presented in a Baroque way can be found throughout the area, some of them being built well into the 1730s. Clarendon Park House (now empty), sitting at the centre of the Clarendon Park Estate on the east side of Salisbury, is an example of a large country house in this style (not so large now, as the wings have been demolished). Despite its Baroque style it is believed to have been completed as late as 1737.[3] Other examples near Salisbury are

3. According to a report of RCHM of 1971 (at the National Monuments Record) the date of design is "possibly 1717".

44. No.1 Castle Street, Salisbury (early 18th century) – jolly, provincial Baroque (shortened by two bays on the left in 1858 to make way for the Market House)

Netherhampton House, with what Pevsner calls its "amazing" façade of about 1710-20 and the Manor House of c.1730 which stands in the main street of Winterbourne Dauntsey but with a curiously urban appearance. In Salisbury itself, there is a rather jolly example of early 18th-century Baroque, No.1 Castle Street (fig.44), which could easily be by the same designer as Myles Place but operating in a more light-hearted mood. Devizes has quite a collection of early 18th-century Baroque houses, notably Brownston House of about 1720, No.16 Market Place, of a few years later, and Greystone House of about 1737. The delightful building known as General Wolfe's House, No.5 Trim Street, Bath (fig.45) is also from this period as is Druce's Hill House, Bradford-on-Avon. General Wolfe's House is an illustration of the difficulty of trying to pin down what is meant by 'Palladian'. It is often so described but, compared with the work of the 'Burlingtonians' whom we shall meet in the next chapter or, indeed, of John Wood, it comes across as rather delicate and insufficiently 'masculine'. More importantly, it lacks a *piano nobile* as well as the high proportion of wall to window that were to be the hallmarks of the Palladian house. Another interesting example of this period in Bath is the former house in Abbey Square (fig.46) which stands to the right of 'Marshal Wade's House' (The National Trust shop) and with an address of No.14 Cheap Street (or No.15 Abbey Square). It is probably by Thomas Greenway and anticipates the use of different classical orders (Doric, Ionic and Corinthian) in its three principal floors that John Wood the Elder would famously use at the King's Circus.

In a more outwardly Baroque style is Biddesden House, east of Ludgershall – "a very remarkable House", Pevsner calls it – built in 1711-12 for General Webb. Westbury House, on its prominent site near the Town Bridge in Bradford-on-Avon, is in the Baroque idiom and so too is the surprising Rosewell House in Kingsmead Square in Bath (fig.9, p.25) which provides such a startling contrast to the more demure classicism of the surrounding streets. This has the remarkably late date of 1736 – the year in which John Wood's Queen Square was being completed and it is as if it were a deliberate counter-blast to Wood's Palladian correctness. It has long been attributed to John Strahan, who did a great deal of work in Bristol

45. *No.5 Trim Street, Bath (early 18th century)*

46. *Marshal Wade's House (left) and No.15 Abbey Square, Bath (both early 18th century)*

47 *&* **48**. *Widcombe Manor, Bath (above and detail, right) (c.1727)*

in a personal, but broadly Palladian, style. He was laying out Beaufort Square at the same time as Wood was building Queen Square, and this remains a well-mannered contribution to Bath's architecture in a neat Palladian style if in a somewhat less impressive form than Queen Square. "Can it really be by John Strahan?" asks Pevsner. It does seem a very peculiar contrast to his other work nearby. It is therefore a relief to find that Tim Mowl has demonstrated that it must be by William Halfpenny who also built a house with many similar features at Queen Charlotte Street, Bristol.[4] Halfpenny also worked in Bristol but his work is of variable quality and he is best known as a writer of pattern books.

49. No.42 Cricklade Street, Swindon (early 18th century)

Ivy House, Chippenham (1730) is another impressive example of a Baroque house built while Queen Square was under construction. The pair of buildings in St John's Court, Sawclose in Bath ('Beau Nash's House' and the slightly earlier building to the south which now forms part of the Theatre Royal and The Garrick's Head) were designed by Thomas Greenway and built early in the 1720s. They have lost much of their original enrichment but are still over-elaborate by the normal standards of Bath. Greenway has also been credited with Widcombe Manor House (c.1727) (figs.47 and 48) just beyond what was then the southern edge of Bath (though Ison doubts if Greenway was capable of it). This, in turn, has a marked similarity to a smaller, but equally elaborate, house in Swindon (now offices), No.42 Cricklade Street (fig.49). Could the same hand be in the design?

4. See his book *To Build The Second City, Architects and Craftsmen of Georgian Bristol* (Redcliffe Press, Bristol, 1991)

50. *No.68 Fore Street, Trowbridge (c.1730)*

Other buildings of this period which are as difficult to categorise as General Wolfe's House but which, like that building, are fine examples of classical design regardless of whether they are 'Baroque', 'Palladian' or anything else, are to be found in Trowbridge and Salisbury. First, are a cluster of buildings in the centre of Trowbridge, all in Bath stone, in Fore Street, which includes The Parade, and continues to curve elegantly through about ninety degrees. Pevsner is in uncharacteristically joyous mood here, describing The Parade as "a stretch of palaces" and the Lloyds TSB Bank building in Fore Street (c.1730) as "so grand as to call to mind Genoa". The carving of the masonry, especially on the cornice and the panels, is of a richness that is rare outside Bath. There is more enrichment to be found on several of the buildings in The Parade but Lloyds TSB's near neighbour, the HSBC Bank building, relies more on good proportions and a careful arrangement of its elements for its imposing presence. This part of Trowbridge is certainly an unexpected pleasure so close to the beer and sausage production plants and to the wasteland around County Hall. As delightful as any is No.68 Fore Street which forms part of The Parade and is the registered office of Usher's Brewery (fig.50). Its unusual arrangement of long, narrow windows flanking the central features can also be found in The Courts at the nearby village of Holt. The wealth for these grand 18th-century houses – and it was as houses that they were built – came from the cloth-making industry that was still going strong in this part of Wiltshire.

51. The Council House, Bourne Hill, Salisbury (re-fashioned mid-18th century)

Though very different from these Trowbridge examples, another attractive building which must be regarded as pre-Palladian is The Council House, Bourne Hill, Salisbury. It has been used as Council offices and committee rooms since 1927 after it was acquired from the Wyndham family in whose possession it had been since 1660. The site adjoins St.Edmund's Church and buildings had been on the site since the 13th century when the College of St.Edmund was founded. What one sees today (fig.51) is a building of the 16th century drastically re-shaped in the middle of the 18th century. It is in brick but contains a lively array of stone dressings including a row of large stone balls on the parapet. Equally lively are the protruding end bays each displaying three different styles of window: a short one on the ground floor (giving it the appearance of a cellar), a large, round-headed one on the first floor and an *oeil de boeuf* window on the top floor. Stylistically, it could almost belong to the middle of the 17th century were it not for the dressings in the style of James Gibbs (1682-1754). Later on, we shall see 'Gibbsian' door and window surrounds in buildings of an unmistakably mid-18th-century character, so it interesting to see them here in a somewhat different setting before we embark on the neo-Palladian era. James Gibbs himself was an independently-minded architect who designed in whatever classical style he thought appropriate, regardless of the pressures put on him to conform to the dictates of Palladianism. His influence on architectural practice was probably greater than that of any of the neo-Palladians, not only on account of superlative works like St.Martin's-in-the-Fields and the Radcliffe Camera, Oxford but through his important pattern books. Though he belonged to no school, the style of surround which bears his name does, as it happens, have clear Palladian origins.

52. *Doorway by Sir Christopher Wren from Longleat House incorporated in 1707 into Lord Weymouth's Grammar School, Warminster*

The church tower of St.Edmund's is a reminder that not all buildings after the introduction of classicism into England were in the classical style. For it was built between 1653 and 1655, being one of the few church buildings in England erected during the period of the Commonwealth. It is no surprise that Tudor Gothic should continue to be used in England until late into the 16th century, but the use of Gothic in the 17th century is much rarer. Its use here is explained by the fact that the tower was built to replace a medieval one that had fallen down, though the earlier tower had stood at the crossing of a much larger church (which had largely disappeared since the Dissolution). So the new tower stands at the west end of a church (now an arts centre) formed from the chancel of the original church. The tower is a sensitive and intelligent piece of work built at a time when the classical style was firmly established. Far less explicable is the design of the Hungerford Almshouses and School in Corsham. This was built in 1668 in golden limestone and could only have been intended as a nostalgic piece of old world charm, built in a homely Perpendicular Gothic style with gables and mullions and some round-headed windows in a Gothic style of its own. Even its classical doorway and pediment are of a naive style that might almost have been put there 50 years before. Perhaps its one claim to modernity is its cupola, reminiscent of the College of Matrons, Salisbury, which had yet to be built.

Finally, a word on Sir Christopher Wren, another architect, like Inigo Jones, who has been the victim of a 'popular tendency'. In Salisbury Close alone, three buildings have been wrongly (or wishfully) attributed to him in the past – The College of Matrons, Malmesbury House (west façade) and Wren Hall. However, it is likely he had a hand in the planning of the rather plain classical church of All Saints, Farley (completed in 1690) and, in Warminster, the design of the doorway of Lord Weymouth School (fig.52) is quite plausibly that of Wren. He is known to have been working for Sir James Thynne at Longleat in the 1660s and it seems the doorway proved too narrow and was removed only 40 years or so later and given to the school then being built. But it is little to show for a man who was born in Wiltshire. A better-known work is the elaborate plasterwork which Wren's father undertook in the church at East Knoyle of which he was Rector. This was in about 1639 when Christopher was aged seven.

7 The Palladian Revival and the Early Villas

From the evidence provided by Salisbury Cathedral Close alone, it is clear that, during the early years of the 18th century, English architecture was edging towards a more correct interpretation of the Roman classical style (of the kind that had been seen in the work of Inigo Jones in the previous century) but that most architects were still more comfortable with the Baroque style. Indeed, 'provincial Baroque', as we have already seen, would be in evidence for many years to come, running in parallel with Palladianism. Maybe this stemmed not so much from provincial backwardness as from timidity: better not to play the new Palladian game at all than to play it wrongly and incur contempt. Also, as strange as it may seem to us today, architectural style had become a matter of party politics and the design of a building often reflected the client's political sympathies – Tory or Whig. The Tories, very broadly, comprised the 'old' landed families, who had traditionally been close to the (now waning) power of the monarch, and also the majority of the Anglican clergy, who had aligned themselves with the restored monarchy after 1660. It was the party of reaction which appealed to monarchists, Stuart sympathisers and Catholics. The Whigs were the party of parliamentary democracy and Protestantism, mistrusting 'Popery' and all things foreign. The party appealed to the growing middle class, the traders, the self-made men as well as to those progressive members of the nobility who had supported the Glorious Revolution of 1688. There was an element of Country versus Town in this although some of the greatest country landowners were Whigs. With the arrival of George I from Hanover in 1714, the Whigs were in the ascendancy and grasped the opportunity to reverse the trend they disliked in architecture of the previous 50 years. To their mind, Vanbrugh, Hawksmoor and even Wren had been too influenced by the Baroque architecture of France, Holland and Italy and had departed too far from the lessons that had been handed down by Inigo Jones. As a result, such architects were often associated with Toryism.

It is one of the leading Whigs, Anthony Ashley Cooper, 3rd Earl of Shaftesbury (1671-1713), who is often credited with the first open attack on the pervading architectural style of his time and with a call for a 'national architecture' reflecting English 'liberty' in politics, religion and social organisation. He was not specific about what the new style should be and it was left to other prominent Whigs to determine what style best expressed the national spirit. The central figure here was Richard Boyle, 3rd Earl of Burlington (1694-1753). He was not merely an active patron of the arts and of architecture in particular but actually turned himself into an architect, something that would have caused a few raised eyebrows among his peers in an age in which being a member of the landed gentry, with its opportunities for patronage, was itself regarded as being a worthy calling. As a young man, he had undertaken an extensive Grand Tour but had taken little, if any, notice of Palladio and his works. But by the age of 25 he had become converted to the cause of Palladianism and set off to Italy again – this time to Vicenza to see the works of Palladio for himself.

What had influenced him were two written works: Colen Campbell's *Vitruvius Britannicus* and Giacomo Leoni's version of *I Quattro Libri*. (Both are dated 1715, though Rudolf Wittkower[1] has shown that Leoni's book was probably published in 1716 but that he had been anxious not to be seen to have lost out to Campbell in a race to produce a book that would appeal to the Whig cognoscenti.) Before leaving for Italy, he had started work on Burlington House in Piccadilly. Campbell acted as his architect[2] but Burlington was an active and much-involved client. Following his return, freshly inspired by close study of Palladio's buildings and armed with many architectural works (including several copies of *I Quattro Libri*) and with a collection of Palladio's drawings, it was only a short step to the undertaking of his own designs for a few select clients or, as in the case of the York Assembly Rooms, when invited to do so by a public body.

One of those for whom he prepared designs was his brother-in-law Charles, Lord Bruce, later Earl of Ailesbury, whose seat was at Tottenham House, Wiltshire, on the southern edge of Savernake Forest. Lord Bruce had married Burlington's sister, Juliana, in 1720 and shortly after the wedding Burlington undertook the designs for a new house in the style of a Palladian villa. The 'executant architect' was Henry Flitcroft, who will appear again in relation to Stourhead. Tottenham House today comprises a much larger classical mansion designed by Thomas Cundy in c.1823-6 which entirely swallowed up the original villa. But the designs which have survived (fig.53) are most interesting in that, apart from drawing on Palladio, there appears to be a clear reference to Wilton House in its corner towers. This was a feature that was to re-occur in several important Palladian Revival designs, including Campbell's Houghton Hall, Norfolk (though when executed after Campbell's death, their pitched roofs were replaced by domes to the design of James Gibbs) and at Holkham Hall, Norfolk (nominally designed by William Kent but probably under the strong influence of Burlington) and we shall see it again at Lydiard Tregoze. It is interesting that the south front of Wilton House should have proved so influential when what was eventually built in Jones's time was a truncated version of a much larger scheme and its corner towers were merely reflecting an existing Tudor feature of the building.

1. See his *Palladio and English Palladianism*
2. He had originally employed James Gibbs. Worsley argues that it was almost certainly Campbell himself who persuaded Burlington to dismiss him, that Gibbs was the only architect Campbell attacked in *Vitruvius Britannicus* (not by name but by implication) and that Campbell had been responsible for his earlier dismissal as one of the two surveyors to the Fifty New Church Commisioners (for London) by disclosing that Gibbs was a catholic.

53. *Tottenham House, Savernake (Lord Burlington, 1720): Henry Flitcroft's drawing of the entrance front. (Devonshire Collection, Chatsworth)*

It has been claimed that Burlington was also responsible for the attractive building, now the National Trust shop, in the Abbey Square, Bath usually called 'Marshal Wade's House'. It was built for the then General Wade in about 1720. He became Bath's MP in 1724 and fought for the Hanoverian side in the 1745 Jacobite Rebellion, being by then a Field Marshal. Burlington had designed a house for him in London in 1723 and this appears to be the only grounds for attributing the house in Bath to Burlington as well. But the use of giant pilasters in this way (fig.46, p.59), as effective and attractive as it may be, is not a device Burlington used elsewhere and the 'incorrect' use of an odd number of pilasters (meaning that one of them divides the façade down the middle) is a feature that Burlington himself is unlikely to have tolerated.

The most important and influential architect of the Palladian Revival was Colen Campbell (1673-1729). He was born and educated in Scotland, a part of Britain which would, from now on, exert a strong influence on the way classicism developed. (For example, both James Gibbs and the Bristol architect, John Strahan, who have both already been mentioned, were from

Scotland.) Little is known about his early life, though it seems that he had practised as a lawyer in Scotland before turning to architecture. It is likely that his conversion to the style of Palladio and Jones was derived partly from another Scottish architect, James Smith, demonstrating that we should no longer speak just of English architecture.

It was Campbell who developed a particular interest in Palladio's villas. These had been built for Venetian gentlemen as country retreats from which they could manage their farms. They did not need to be too large because the owner would often have a palazzo in Venice or one of the other cities in the region. What Palladio gave them was a country house in the same basic form that can be seen throughout the European countries of the western Mediterranean (with a good basement and 1½ or 2½ floors above with small window openings, the uppermost windows in the 'half' floor being either square or even shorter than their width) but fashionably enhanced by rooms laid out and proportioned according to Vitruvian principles and provided with enough Roman architectural details to make it imposing and important. This was often achieved by giving a temple-like front to the building, a device Palladio was the first architect to employ. He justified this in *I Quattro Libri* by expressing the view that such temple fronts "show the entrance to the house, and add very much to the grandeur and magnificence of the work, the front bay thus made more eminent than the rest; besides they are very commodious for placing the ensigns or arms of the owners, which are commonly put in the middle of the front". He goes on to suggest the ancients "very probably took the invention and principles of them from private ... houses". We now know that this was a fallacy but porticos continued to be an essential feature of the country house even after the fallacy had been exposed. In the countryside, the central bulk of the villa, containing both the living quarters and service accommodation, was normally flanked by wings containing space for the storage and processing of farm produce or even for keeping animals. The form of these wings were also developed from the traditional form of farmhouse that can still be seen all over the Veneto region, namely a basic block of the type previously described and, attached to it, a lower arcaded building with a number of simple arches, commonly three.

Between 1715 and 1724 Campbell produced a handful of designs for town or country villas that would serve as influential models for the Palladian movement – Wanstead House, Essex (for which three different designs survive), Houghton in Norfolk, Mereworth in Kent, Lord Herbert's House in Whitehall, Newby in Yorkshire and, in 1721, Stourhead House in Wiltshire.

The manor of Stourton was purchased in 1717 by Henry Hoare (1672-1725), the son of Richard Hoare, the founder of Hoare's Bank. The fact that the bank still trades in the City of London is some indication that Henry Hoare himself did not give up his commercial interests when he acquired

54. *Stourhead House (Colen Campbell, 1720-24): design published in* Vitruvius Britannicus

his country estate. What he required, like many of his contemporaries, was not so much a country house but more a house in the country which would serve as a rural outlet from his concerns in the City. Thus it was not merely the form of the Palladian villa that appealed to the Whig gentlemen of the 18th century but its very function and Campbell had been quick to recognise this. His appointment as the architect of Stourhead was not a surprising one. First, Lord Burlington was a client of Hoare's Bank and Campbell's would have been the name that he would have suggested to Henry Hoare had he been consulted. Second, Henry Hoare had married the daughter of Sir William Benson who had been appointed as Surveyor of the King's Works in 1718. As his Deputy, he had appointed Colen Campbell and would have had sufficient confidence in him to recommend him to his brother-in-law.

Campbell's design for Stourhead House (figs.54 and 55), which was begun in c.1721, possibly exemplifies the characteristic features of the Palladian villa better than any other building in Britain. Its internal layout followed Palladio's precepts with a perfect cube at its centre and rooms leading off it with one or other of the recommended proportions that we saw in Chapter 2. The service rooms and servants' quarters were in the raised basement, the principal rooms on the main floor above (the *piano nobile*) and bedrooms in a first floor of lower height. And that is all. This is no Chatsworth or Petworth, let alone a Blenheim Palace. The basement level is indicated by rustication, the outer ground-floor windows are set in tabernacle frames and the first-floor windows are more modest both in form and size. The design of the façade is neatly finished off with a balustrade

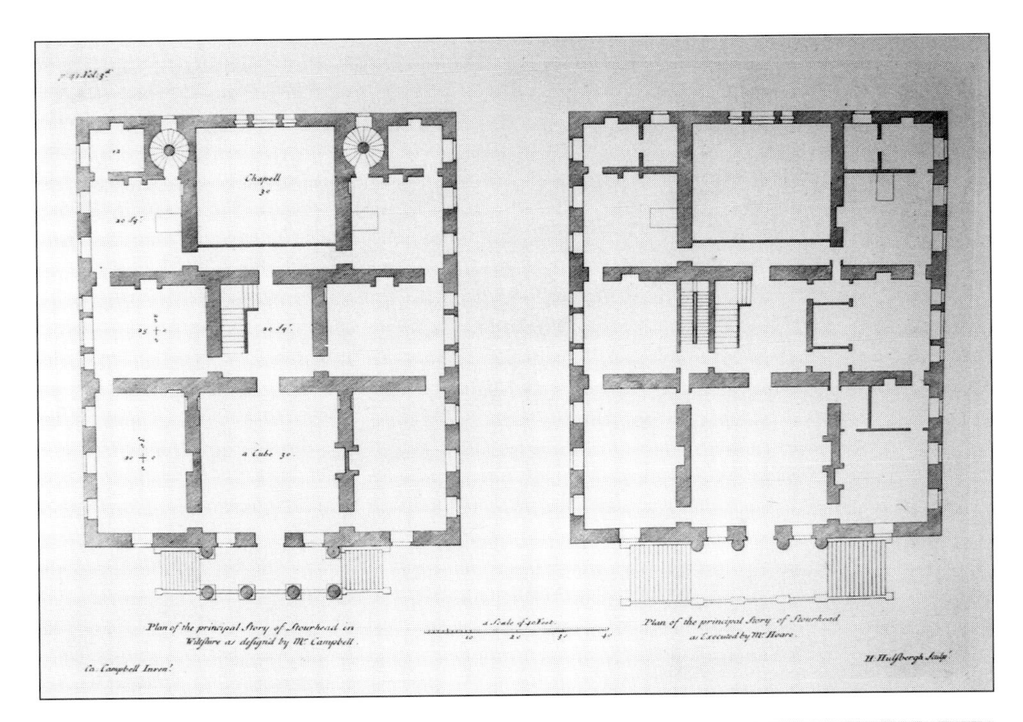

55. *Stourhead House (Colen Campbell, 1720-24): design for the interior published in* Vitruvius Britannicus

with ball ornaments and statues breaking the skyline. The only note of grandeur lies in the central open portico, though even this may have been too much for the client because the design, as executed, omitted the four Corinthian columns and substituted more self-effacing engaged columns with a triangular pediment above (fig.56). Campbell's original design (with some alterations) was only carried out three generations later, in 1838, by Sir Henry Hugh Hoare to the design of Charles Parker, a pupil of Sir Jeffry Wyatville. The wings were added in the 1790s by Sir Richard Colt Hoare

56. *Stourhead House (Colen Campbell, 1720-24, with later additions and rebuilding)*

to a design (that may have been his own) that carefully reflects that of the original house. In 1902, the main block was gutted by fire but carefully rebuilt to Campbell's design by a local architect Doran Webb acting on the instructions of Sir Henry Hoare, 6th Baronet, who had inherited the estate in 1894. The builder of the original house was a local man, Nathaniel Ireson, who was himself such an experienced building practitioner that he may well have acted as executant architect. Indeed, he had a small local architectural practice in Somerset; his own designs were broadly neo-Palladian though he was responsible for the design of the splendid Baroque-style Ven House that can be seen on the road between Sherborne and Shaftesbury in Dorset (where it passes through a corner of Somerset). He is buried in the churchyard of Wincanton parish church, just over the border in Somerset, and even his tomb and memorial statue were of his own making!

It is necessary to return to Sir William Benson because he had been responsible for the design of a house in Wiltshire that is nowadays regarded as the very first example of a Palladian Revival villa in Britain. In 1709, he had bought the manor of Newton Toney from the family of Celia Fiennes, the famous traveller. In the previous year, he had taken a lease (from Lord Bruce – who would soon be employing Lord Burlington at Tottenham House) of Amesbury Abbey and he was a frequent visitor to Wilton House. He would therefore have been familiar with these two Palladian works (which were both, at that time, thought to be exclusively the work of Inigo Jones) and he was anxious to emulate them with one of his own design. In 1710, while High Sheriff of Wiltshire, he demolished the old house at Newton Tony and began building a new house that he would call 'Wilbury Manor' a composite name referring to the two buildings that had inspired him.

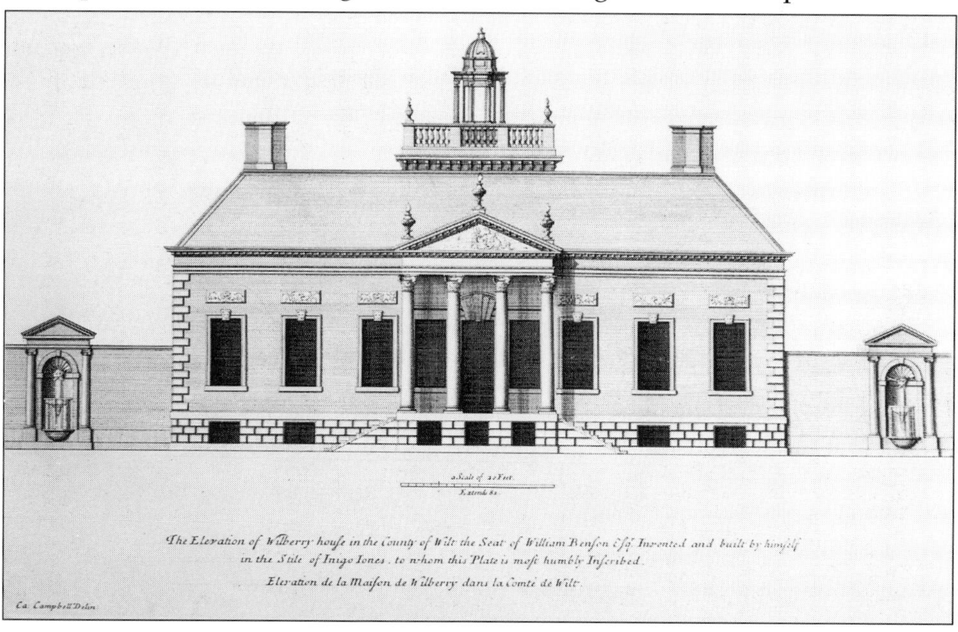

57. *Wilbury Manor (Sir William Benson, c.1710): design published in* Vitruvius Britannicus

Thanks to Colen Campbell's illustration in *Vitruvius Britannicus* (fig.57) we have a record of the original design though the house itself has changed out of all recognition. It is a remarkable design and of great historical importance. So who exactly was William Benson? Summerson, in a typically trenchant comment, calls him "a poet and pamphleteer with some knowledge of architecture" and asserts that when in 1714 he was appointed Surveyor of the Royal Works to succeed Sir Christopher Wren (after Vanbrugh had declined the post) "he proved his incompetence with surprising promptitude" and resigned in 1719. He had been at the Court of Hanover in the years before his appointment, working (like Isaac de Caus at Wilton) on fountains and other elaborate water works and perhaps lost no opportunity to press his case with the future King for his appointment as Surveyor.

Was the design really Benson's or was Campbell, whom Benson had appointed as his Deputy in 1714, being suitably deferential in *Vitruvius Britannicus* describing it as "invented and built" by Benson "in the style of Inigo Jones" when he himself had been the 'inventor'? Or, as Worsley suggests, was the hand of William Talman (the distinguished architect whom Benson knew well) in the design? It is still a bit of a mystery.

There is another local Palladian venture involving Benson that ought to be mentioned. His brother-in-law, Henry Hoare (of Stourhead), also owned Quarley, the manor adjoining Newton Toney to the east, just inside Hampshire. In 1723, they were responsible for the insertion of a new Venetian window in the east end of Quarley's parish church (fig.58). It contains a carved inscription:

GULIELMUS BENSON & HENRICUS HOARE ARM: F.A.D.1723

on the outside and the same inscription, but with the names reversed, on the inside. The side lights of the window have since been filled in.

58. *St.Michael and All Angels, Quarley, Hampshire: Benson and Hoare's Venetian window (1723)*

8 The Palladian Revival and Bath

Andrea Palladio had plenty of advice to give about villas and 'temples' but had nothing helpful to say about the design of towns or streets. So, while street design was to become an important element of the Palladian Revival, it was influenced far more by experience gained in England, from Inigo Jones onwards, than by Palladio himself. In London, Jones's terraces at Covent Garden and Lincoln's Inn Fields were the earliest home-grown attempts at urban design in classical form. Later in the 17th century, Bloomsbury Square became the first development that could be called a 'square' and this was followed early in the 18th century by Grosvenor Square.

At about this time, the need arose in Bath for new fashionable living accommodation as its waters and its social life became an increasing draw to people 'of quality'. Beau Nash, Bath's 'King' and Master of Ceremonies, had worked hard to introduce civilised codes of behaviour and a pattern of social rounds and entertainment that were to establish Bath as the pre-eminent resort spa in the country. It fell to John Wood (1704-54) to establish equally civilised standards for the various buildings that would be required. We shall see how he was capable of designing individual dwellings that could stand comparison with the best of his contemporary architects but his great achievement was that, unlike them, he succeeded in designing an acceptable form of 'mass housing' (if hardly houses for the masses).

His work would be carried on by his equally talented son, also called John Wood; thus they are usually referred to as the Elder and Younger. John Wood the Elder was often referred to, in times nearer his own, as 'John Wood of Bath'. This may simply have been in recognition of the fact that most of his professional life was spent in Bath and that his best-known works are to be found there (Queen Square and the King's Circus). But it is more likely that as, for example, with the painter, Joseph Wright of Derby, the label infers the damning crime of provincialism. If so, the inference was largely misplaced for, after working for Lord Bingley in Yorkshire (probably on the recommendation of a member of the nobility in Bath who had recognised Wood's talents), he went on to work in London for Lord Chandos. He was still only in his early twenties and was probably working in a minor or subordinate capacity (there is no record of his work there) but he would have been introduced to the new neo-Palladian style and perhaps met some of the leading architects including Campbell; he would have seen current building projects including Grosvenor Square. Even after he finally settled in Bath, in 1727, he was invited to undertake major commissions in Liverpool, at Llandaff Cathedral and in Bristol.

On his return to Bath, his London connections and influences were brought to bear without delay. His first major work was a rebuilding of St.John's Hospital ('hospital', that is, in the sense of almshouses) for his

59. St.John's Hospital, Bath (John Wood the Elder, 1727)

London patron Lord Chandos who, despite constant complaints about workmanship and water closets, engaged Wood on other related work. Many of Wood's buildings of this period have been demolished but the Hospital itself (of which Wood built the northern and eastern ranges) survives and is a pleasant spot to visit with its quiet courtyard between the west end of Bath Street and Westgate Buildings. Architecturally, Wood's buildings appear to have been heavily influenced by Colen Campbell's terraced houses at Old Burlington Street (see figs.59 and 60). This is the simplicity of the Palladian country villa brought into the town but without any grand central feature (such as we have seen at Stourhead). Already we

60. Old Burlington Street, London.
(© Crown copyright, N.M.R.)

***61**. Ralph Allen's House, North Parade Passage, Bath (John Wood the Elder, 1727)*

are starting to see those characteristics that we now take for granted in the Georgian terrace – rhythms and proportions deriving from classical precepts but with a minimum of specific Roman architectural features.

But he would soon have a chance to exercise his skills in the use of such features. In the same year, 1727, he provided the design for a town house for the wealthy Bath patron Ralph Allen. Allen, a Cornishman who had come to Bath in 1710, had already made one fortune from his work on the reorganisation of postal services and would soon make another from the development of stone quarries on his land at Combe Down on the south-eastern edge of Bath. He would bring his wealth and entrepreneurial skills to the early stages of Bath's remarkable development to be set alongside the different, but complementary, skills of Richard Nash and John Wood. He had bought a property in North Parade Passage (the narrow street that contains Sally Lunn's House) and, at the back of it and at right-angles to it, proceeded to build a three-storey extension which would then have appeared as a separate, and very 'showy', house facing east towards the wooded hillside beyond the River Avon. There is some doubt about the degree of Wood's involvement (Ison felt it lacked the normal finesse of his work) but Wood himself[1] described it as a "Sample for the greatest Magnificence that was ever proposed by me for our City Houses". Its narrow front façade (fig.61) is crammed with a wealth of classical features in the Palladian style including a Venetian window comprising, in effect, the entire width of the *piano nobile*, its three elements tucked between four giant Corinthian engaged columns rising into the storey above. The whole effect is more like that of a doll's house[2]

1. See his book, *An Essay Towards A Description of Bath* (1742)
2. It is not unlike Queen Mary's doll's house on display at Windsor Castle.

62. No.24 High Street, Chippenham (John Wood the Elder?) before the removal of the façade to Bath in 1933. (© Crown copyright, N.M.R.)

than a real one especially now that it is surrounded by later development and can only be glimpsed, somewhat surrealistically, down narrow passages. Throughout Allen's lifetime, however, the view to the hills remained unimpeded and 25 years later (1762) he decided to grace the view with a folly, Sham Castle; its design is attributed to Richard Jones and is still an eye-catcher from the centre of Bath (especially when it is floodlit). The building of Allen's house was not without its detriment to the ordinary citizens of Bath. In *An Essay Towards a Description of Bath*, Wood reports that

> a third Part of the Bowling Green having been granted for a Garden to the House, Smock Racing and Pig Racing, playing at Foot-Ball and running with the Feet in Bags in that Green, four of the Bath Diversions of those Days, thereby received their Final End: Nor did Grinning, Stareing, Scolding, Eating Hot Furmety, Laughing, Whistling and Jiging upon the Stage for Rings, Shirts, Smocks, Hats, Etc. escape the common Ruin; these Amusements falling likewise.

The list does not include playing musical chairs but that has been the fate of a house façade, not unlike that of Ralph Allen's house, that has been traditionally attributed to John Wood and so is best mentioned here. The story involves Chippenham, a town that was once known as 'Little Bath' for its splendid buildings in Bath stone; but the number of those buildings has sadly diminished through redevelopment. The saddest loss was No.24 High Street to make way for a shop in 1933 (fig.62). In one of its 'Obituaries of Buildings' in that year, the *Architecture and Building News* reported that the house had been bought with a view to preservation and re-erection elsewhere and that according to tradition the façade was the central elevation of a house at Bowden Hill built about 1740 "but this is by no means more certain than it is, as some think, the work of John Wood". The benefactor of this second removal was Ernest Cook (grandson of the founder of Thomas Cook & Sons) who had purchased No.1 Sion Hill Place in Bath and incorporated the Chippenham building into the western façade, making a rich contrast with Pinch's plainer design of the southern façade (see Chapter 16). The proportions were slightly altered by the insertion of two additional courses of stone but what makes it interesting for our present purposes is the similarity of the Palladian design to Ralph Allen's house, especially the window arrangement within the giant engaged columns.

Now, even while he was in Yorkshire, John Wood had begun to dream about Bath's potential and to plan for its future development according to his own ideas. He drew designs for, first, "a grand Place of Assembly, to be called the Royal Forum of Bath"; second, "another Place, no less magnificent, for the Exhibition of Sports, to be called the Grand Circus"; and finally, "a third Place, of equal State with either of the former, for the Practice of medicinal Exercises, to be called the Imperial Gymnasium of the City." His enthusiasm stemmed from a belief that Bath was the *Troy Novant* of ancient legend and once contained such splendours. His obsessions have been subjected to a careful and fascinating study by Tim Mowl and Brian Earnshaw[3] and, since Wood was a far better architect than antiquary, it would be better here to concentrate on the architecture! Suffice it to say, he showed his designs to two Bath landowners, a London surgeon, John Gay, and Lord Essex but neither saw fit to embrace his ideas with any enthusiasm. Nothing daunted, he began another project which was neither Forum, Circus nor Gymnasium but was still a major, and important scheme of his own conception and design, namely Queen Square, begun in 1728. He secured the land in stages from John Gay (whose name lives on in Gay Street) and, through a system of building leases, was able to control the outward design of all four sides of the Square. In other words, he acted as the co-ordinating developer as well as architect while individual lessees were able to build to their, or their clients', own requirements behind Wood's street façades, a pattern that would be followed time and time again in Bath by Wood and those that followed him. As he proceeded with the development of Queen Square, he was forced into a few compromises through cost constraints but, in general, his vision was achieved. Earlier attempts in London to form town squares were, by comparison, poorly co-ordinated and far less visually cohesive.

It is difficult today for the visitor to Bath to grasp the historical importance of Queen Square. Apart from the press of modern traffic, so different from the carriages and sedan chairs for which Bath's streets were designed to

3. See *John Wood, Architect of Obsession*.

63. Queen Square, Bath, north side (John Wood the Elder, begun 1728)

cater, the character of the square is destroyed by the trees which have been planted in later times (once the leaves are out, no more than two sides of the square can be seen properly from any point); and the very fact that Queen Square was to prove such an influential model means that it now almost appears commonplace. Most of Wood's skill was directed to the north side (fig.63), made to look like a single building but in fact comprising seven houses. (Its intended palace-like appearance is now marred by a thick growth of creeper at the western end.) Its design is so similar to Peckwater Quadrangle at Christ Church, Oxford (built between 1706 and 1714) (fig.64) that this must have been the main source of Wood's inspiration. There is little to distinguish between the two designs as regards the treatment of the ground floor rustication and key stones, the tabernacle windows of the *piano nobile* with alternating curved and triangular heads, the slightly projecting central five bays with six engaged columns supporting a pediment and, lastly, the use of giant pilasters along the main façade. The quadrangle had been built more than 20 years earlier to a design by Henry Aldrich, the Dean of Christ Church. Summerson is a little sniffy about the Aldrich design

64. Peckwater Quadrangle, Christ Church, Oxford (Henry Aldrich, 1706-14). (The Governing Body of Christ Church, Oxford)

suggesting that the triple repetition of the design theme and the "banal" junction of the centre with the two side wings "declare the design an amateur's conception". So where does this leave Wood's design as it obviously has so much in common? The fundamental difference (which entirely by-passes Summerson's strictures) is that Wood has used the design for a single, free-standing side of a town square without the enclosing wings more appropriate for a college quadrangle. And to compensate for the loss of the wings, he has turned three outside bays at each end into pavilions with their own slight projection and engaged columns. Finally, Wood has preferred the rather grander Corinthian order to Aldrich's Ionic. The difficult question arises once again – is it truly 'Palladian' if it appears to derive from a design of 1705 which is normally regarded as an age still within the grip of the Baroque?[4] First, Summerson (and who would ever wish to disagree with Summerson?) concludes his comments on Peckwater Quadrangle by suggesting that "the Palladian restraint of the whole is, however, remarkable for its date" (showing again that Campbell and Burlington should not be exclusively credited with instigating the Palladian Revival) and second, Wood has skilfully brought other precedents to bear, not least (and not for the last time, as we shall see) one of Campbell's Wanstead House designs. And, once again, we find a *piano nobile*, relatively small windows and a reliance on the use of the orders rather than elaborate decoration. So with some confidence we can say "yes" to the question "Is it Palladian?". In any event, Wood's Palladian credentials are confirmed by his name appearing

4. For example, Peckwater Quadrangle is dealt with in Doreen Yarwood's *The Architecture of Britain* in the chapter on 'The English Baroque 1690-1730' rather than the one on 'Gibbs and the English Palladians 1710-1760', illustrating the impossibility of neat categorisation.

amongst the subscribers to Isaac Ware's 1738 edition of *I Quattro Libri* (replacing Leoni's unreliable 1715 version) alongside those of Lord Burlington, Lord Pembroke, Henry Flitcroft and Matthew Brettingham, all active supporters of the Palladian Revival.

The buildings on the other three sides of Queen Square were intended as plainer foils to the more impressive north side, giving the spectator of the scene a satisfying mixture of grandeur and restraint – everything in moderation, nothing to excess. In essence, though each side is slightly different from each other, each is simply an astylar version of the north side, echoing its general form and its treatment of the doors and windows, in a style reminiscent of Wood's work at St.John's Hospital. Only the west side has undergone any significant change since Wood's day: its centre was originally open to take a recessed mansion but the gap was later filled (by a Greek Revival building designed by John Pinch the Younger) so that the west side now comprises a complete terrace like the others.

We saw in Chapter 6 that while Wood was building Queen Square, other new houses, designed by John Strahan, were being built a little to the south in Kingsmead Square and Beaufort Square. They suffer from any comparison with Queen Square, lacking its style and grandeur (as well as its scale), but they are a pleasant enough addition to Bath that most other towns would be delighted to possess.

Thus the Palladian character of the fast expanding city became established and we shall see in later chapters how this character was maintained.

9 The Revival Continues – More Villas and a Bridge

So we have seen some important early examples of neo-Palladianism at Wilbury Manor, Tottenham House and Stourhead House and, in Bath, some early work by John Wood that would have an immense influence on the development of that city as well as on urban development elsewhere. And this is all before 1730 while the new style was still a novelty and not yet entirely accepted as the 'national style' in the way that Lord Burlington had hoped. The 1730s might well have seen a widespread reaction against what was, after all, a foreign import (leaving aside the contribution of Inigo Jones) and a return to the freer classicism of Vanbrugh and Hawksmoor or even to the more home-spun style that we have seen in Salisbury Close and which gave us some of England's finest buildings. But the decade proved to be one of consolidation and advance for neo-Palladianism.

In 1731, work began on a new house at Standlynch (between Salisbury and Downton) for Sir Peter Vandeput. The house, originally known as Standlynch House, was re-named Trafalgar House after it had been given by 'a grateful nation' to the heirs of Lord Nelson. Now known as Trafalgar Park it is being developed as a centre for musical studies. Sir Peter was a wealthy merchant of Dutch descent who had acquired the Standlynch estate in 1725. His daughter had married the architect Roger Morris and the house had long been attributed to him. In 1986, Sally Jeffery published evidence[1] that the true architect was John James (c.1672-1746), the son of the Rev.John James from Hampshire and a serious student of architecture; in 1708 he translated a treatise on the *Five Orders of Columns*, by Perrault, and in 1710 had published an Italian treatise on perspective. He was the architect of St.George's Church, Hanover Square (1712-24), which was to be an influence on Hawksmoor and Gibbs. He became the beneficiary of Campbell's attack on James Gibbs by succeeding Gibbs as one of the two surveyors to the Fifty New Church Commissioners (for London). In 1718 he joined Vanbrugh as a Joint Clerk of Works at Greenwich Hospital (explaining why he is often referred to as 'John James of Greenwich'). Appledurcombe House, Isle of Wight, was one of his early designs and his design for a house at Wricklemarsh, Kent, was included by Colen Campbell in *Vitruvius Britannicus*. Colvin summarises James's career thus:

> James was a competent architect, but he lacked inventive fancy, and the buildings are for the most part plain, unadorned and somewhat stolid ... James must be regarded as a rather sober disciple of Wren and Vanbrugh rather than as an effective pioneer of Palladianism.

1. See an article in *Country Life* ('An Architect for Standlynch House') 13 February 1986; see also *Country Life* articles by Giles Worsley about Trafalgar Park of 3 and 10 April 1997.

65. Trafalgar House, Standlynch (central block only, without porch, John James, 1731)

Colvin would not have known of the attribution of Standlynch to James when he wrote these words so it will be interesting to see if they ring true. James's inspiration was Inigo Jones rather than Palladio and what he produced at Standlynch (fig.65), whilst it can be called a villa, is certainly very different from those of Campbell or Lord Burlington. It needs to be visualised without the wings or the portico which were added later (see Chapter 13). We are left with a plain brick box relieved only by rusticated quoins and window surrounds (the door, now hidden by the portico, is of the same style) and a heavy cornice. There is no *piano nobile* and the windows are of pre-Palladian proportions. Bearing in mind that the attic storey was probably an afterthought on the part of the client, the house was designed to have an appearance much more like that of St.Edmund's College (now The Council House), Salisbury (fig.51, p.63) – though a much duller version of it – than that of any of the villas encountered in Chapter 7. The west-facing front is of the same design but with a pediment rising into the attic storey above the three central bays which are slightly brought forward.

Yet both Palladio and Campbell would have approved of the siting of the house (recommended by James to Sir Peter) with its views across the Avon valley and a noble, if rather distant, presence on the hills above when viewed from the valley bottom. James himself, who had worked at Wilton many years before, was more anxious to pay homage to Inigo Jones than to show any affinity with the neo-Palladians and it is when we enter the house we see the Jonesian contrast at work between the "unaffected" exterior and the inward "imagination and fire". What we step into is an entrance hall, of single-cube proportions, which is all richness and exuberance; for the first time there are columns to be seen, in the form of pilasters of the Composite order, the richest of them all. The chimney-piece, door and window surrounds, frieze and cornice are all richly decorated and, at risk of the effect of the entire scheme collapsing under an excess of elaboration, the walls and the coved ceiling carry a mass of rococo patterns in plasterwork. The fact that it does not collapse is largely due to its monochrome creamy-grey colour scheme. The whole is a small-scale reminder of the rich grandeur of Wilton behind its astylar south front. A plasterwork bust of Inigo Jones (fig.22, p.39) is displayed above the fireplace. One must assume that James had it put there.

Lord Burlington was not the only Earl of his time to treat architecture so seriously as actually to practise it. The other was Henry Herbert (1693-1751), heir to Wilton House and the great Pembroke estate to which he succeeded as 9th Earl in 1733. Following in the Pembroke tradition, he was favourably placed at court, having been appointed Lord of the Bedchamber to the Prince of Wales and, when the Prince became King George II, Groom of the Stole and First Lord of the Bedchamber. He was appointed to a number of prestigious military posts. His pugnacious looks, as captured in a bust by Roubiliac (fig.66)[2] seem to belie his reputation as the 'Architect Earl'. It comes as no surprise to find that, among the sports he indulged in as a young man, he loved boxing or that he could behave very rudely and easily lose his temper. But Wilton would have been fertile ground for any artistic interests the young man may have had to take root in, surrounded by the works of Jones and Webb and no doubt influenced by the tastes of his father who had purchased, and installed at Wilton, the Roman statuary brought back by Lord Arundel from Italy when he was accompanied by

***66**. Bust by Roubiliac of Henry Herbert, 9th Earl of Pembroke.*
(Wilton House Trust)

2. The bust shown here (from his memorial in the Church of St.Mary and St.Nicholas in Wilton) is, strictly speaking, a copy, the original having been sold by the Earl of Pembroke and the proceeds donated to assist with the maintenance of this remarkable 19th-century Italianate church. Another similar bust of the 9th Earl by Roubiliac is in the Gothic Hall at Wilton House.

Inigo Jones. According to Horace Walpole's fanciful opinion, the soul of Inigo Jones had assisted the muses in Herbert's education. "No man", he claimed, "had a purer taste in building than Earl Henry."[3]

Henry Herbert had been a student at Christ Church, Oxford at the time Dean Aldrich was building Peckwater Quadrangle, the pioneering, if flawed, essay in Palladianism noted in the previous chapter. He visited Veneto in 1712 and may well have seen the works of Palladio. His attachment to the Palladian movement was demonstrated, while he was still Lord Herbert, by the appointment of Colen Campbell as architect for his London home, Pembroke House, in Whitehall, completed in 1724. His own first venture in designing was Marble Hill, Twickenham for the Countess of Suffolk, the mistress of George II. In 1730, he designed the Column of Victory in the grounds of Blenheim Palace, a fluted Doric column, 130 ft. high, topped by a lead statue of the Duke of Marlborough by John Cheere. In 1732, he built a house for his own occupation, Westcombe House at Blackheath and in 1737, The White Lodge, Richmond for George II. In between, he had made the mistake of undertaking the building of a house at Wimbledon for the odious Duchess of Marlborough. Not only did she remain dissatisfied with all he tried to do to meet her requirements but spread stories that Herbert was trying to swindle her by using cheaper materials than those for which he charged. So it is not surprising that his next commission was for himself! Between 1735 and 1738 he put up the building for which he is best known – the Palladian Bridge at Wilton (fig.67), "one of the most beautiful buildings in all England ... a superb and eternal work of art."[4] It performs the practical function of a pedestrian link, over the River Nadder, between the two parts of the gardens of the House (which the Earl was reshaping at that time, sweeping away most of de Caus's layout) but it is as an eye-catching feature within the grounds that it is most valued. It was soon copied at Stowe, Prior Park and Hagley. It consists of a covered, open-sided arcade in the Ionic order lifted above the river by an arched, rusticated base and connected to the banks by an elegant flight of steps at each end, partly supported by a further arch. The 'arcade' is, perhaps, more properly described as two open, pedimented, pavilions linked by a covered colonnade. The whole structure, arcade and steps together, has a balustrade along each side. Apart from having a prosaic safety function, these balustrades tie the whole structure together visually and help to emphasise its sculptural qualities. Indeed, it is as a piece of abstract sculpture that the bridge is best regarded. From whatever angle it is viewed, the shape of the bridge is immensely satisfying.[5] Its various elements seem to exist in perfect harmony. The eye can take it in either as a series of horizontal elements (roof and pediments, colonnade

3. Brian Fothergill, in *The Strawberry Hill Set* (Faber, London, 1983).
4. The words of James Lees-Milne in *Earls of Creation*.
5. At Wilton, unfortunately, unlike at Stowe and Prior Park, there is normally no access for visitors to the bridge itself, and therefore no opportunity to experience the sculptural effect from the inside.

67. The Palladian Bridge, Wilton House (9th Earl of Pembroke, 1735-38). (Wilton House Trust)

and pavilions, balustrade, base and steps) or as a series of vertical elements (corresponding to the five arches plus the balustraded areas on the banks).

It is often asserted that the design derives from one of Palladio's (in *I Quattro Libri*) for the Rialto Bridge in Venice to which the design by Giovanni de Ponte was preferred in a competition and was therefore not executed. But it has to be said that the connection is not immediately obvious. The Rialto design is on a vastly greater scale, incorporating, for example, three spacious streets separated by rows of shops. There would have been 72 shops in all, disposed in 6 rows of 12 each side of the streets. It is true it had a pavilion at each end with some similarities to the Wilton design but Palladio's pavilions stood on the banks of the Grand Canal (rather than over it).[6] The principal feature of Palladio's bridge was a central loggia topped by a large pedimented roof whose temple-like fronts would have faced the canal. The bridge itself was carried on three huge semi-circular arches of equal size. These three features, the pavilions on the banks, the central pediments and the three equal arches, are, as we shall see in Chapter 14, substantially shared by the bridge that Robert Adam designed for Bath (Pulteney Bridge), but all three are missing from Wilton.

6. These made the proposal of doubtful practicality in view of the widespread demolition that would have been needed to allow the building of the pavilions and their associated flights of steps – a rare case of Palladio's practical sense and feel for the 'right' solution deserting him.

The main argument in favour of this Palladian precedent being the source of the Wilton bridge is that Henry Herbert was an enthusiastic Palladian, that he can be expected to have looked at *I Quattro Libri* for some guidance and that this is the nearest in appearance to the one that he built. At any rate, the concept was elegantly and divinely simple and must be unique in architectural history in inspiring the building of four virtually exact copies – not only at Stowe, Prior Park and Hagley but even (in 1771) in Russia, at Tsarskoe Selo, near St.Petersburg, for Catherine the Great.

The name that has yet to be mentioned in all this is Roger Morris who had worked with Herbert at all his previous ventures before doing so again at Wilton. Their respective roles have never been entirely clear. Roger Morris (1695-1749) was the son of a carpenter and, in 1724, whilst engaged on speculative house-building in the west end of London, was being described as a bricklayer. After an appointment as Clerk of the Works at Richmond New Park Lodge (1727), he became the Master Carpenter to the Office of Ordnance in 1734. But by then he was certainly undertaking architectural commissions. In 1731, for example, he won a competition for the Council House at Chichester, West Sussex and in 1732 built Whitton House, Twickenham for the Earl of Ilay in a villa style that was very much his own. At Althorp House, Northamptonshire, he built a stable block using, as a central feature, a version of Inigo Jones's Tuscan-style St.Paul's Church, Covent Garden, in a way that was both effective and unprecedented in 18th-century architecture.[7]

Yet Morris seemed to spend much of his time working either as an associate of another architect or as an architectural assistant to members of the aristocracy. He is known, for example, to have assisted Campbell on a number of commissions and to have worked with the Duke of Richmond and the Duke of Argyll as well as with Lord Pembroke. Perhaps his humble origins and lack of a formal education curbed any desire to be a 'grand' architect who could move as an equal with the gentry in Georgian society.

As far as the Bridge is concerned, both Horace Walpole and the antiquary, George Vertue, are on record as regarding Lord Pembroke as the designer. Dean Swift had called him the architect of Marble Hill.[8] It therefore seems likely, though we may never know for sure, that the inspiration for the design of the Palladian Bridge came from Lord Pembroke and that Morris's experience and know-how made sure that the practicality of its construction matched the beauty of its design.

Though it involves jumping ahead a few years, this is a good moment to mention a house in another part of Wiltshire which, though built as a principal family seat, is strongly influenced by the idea of the Palladian villa. This is Lydiard Tregoze, now within Swindon, which derives from a house first built here by a junior branch of the St.John family in the 15th century. Their family tombs, mainly from the 16th and 17th centuries, can

7. The building now houses the exhibition dedicated to the life of Diana, Princess of Wales.
8. See *Earls of Creation* by James Lees-Milne.

68. Lydiard Tregoze House, Swindon (1743): a 'modernised' older version

be seen in the church immediately behind the house; it is a remarkable sight and the finest collection from this period in the county. The house was much larger while these St.Johns were alive and the church served the medieval village of Lydiard Tregoze but, for reasons that are not known, it had disappeared by the 18th century, leaving the house and church in isolation. By then, the owner was John St.John, 2nd Viscount St.John, who in 1743 began a re-structuring of the house which was to give it its present neat and pleasing appearance (fig.68). Being constrained by the former house (parts of which still exist behind the façade) there is no *piano nobile* but in other respects the façade is a piece of correct and unpretentious Palladianism. The corner towers can be taken either as a direct quotation from the villas of Palladio (Villa Emo, for example, or Villa Pisani at Bagnolo (fig.69)) or inspired by Wilton House. It is held together well by the central pediment, the strong cornice, the balustrade and the rusticated quoins, which extend into the upper part of the towers. It has been attributed to Roger Morris – but purely on stylistic grounds as there is not a shred of hard evidence that links him to it. If the St.John family papers were available, both this mystery and that of the missing village, might be cleared up but, early in the Second World War, the family records, about 1½ tons of them, were disposed of as salvage, to help the war effort, by the eccentric 6th Viscount Bolingbroke.[9] The house itself, neglected for several generations, was purchased by Swindon Borough Council during the war and then was heroically restored by that body during

9. Viscount St.John's son became the 3rd Viscount of Bolingbroke. For an amusing account of an encounter with the 6th Viscount see *No Voice From The Hall* by John Harris (Murray, London, 1998).

69. Villani Pisani, Bagnolo (Andrea Palladio, 1542)

the 1950s, at a time when their priorities lay with town expansion to accommodate London overspill. The grounds are now a public park and the house, finely restored, can be visited throughout the year and represents an important resource for the Borough's museum service. In Palladian tradition, the interiors are richer than the plain exterior, the library being especially fine with its original richly carved bookcases, topped by busts of philosophers in open pediments, and a heavily decorated panelled ceiling.

A Palladian villa of more modest proportions is Belcombe Court on the western fringe of Bradford-on-Avon (fig.70). Nowadays it is almost entirely hidden from view by the trees in the garden and a high wall with security gates; but when it was built and designed by John Wood in 1734 for Francis Yerbury on the northern slopes of the Avon valley it was intended to have a delightful view across the valley to the hills and woods beyond. The Yerburys were manufacturers of 'fancy' or twilled woollen cloths and their mill and workers' cottages lay behind the house which was designed to face the other way across the valley. In *An Essay towards a Description of Bath,* Wood explains, in his standard self-aggrandising prose, that the façade of the villa (then called Belcomb Brook) "is adorned with Pilasters of the *Ionick* Order, forming the best Tetrastyle Frontispiece, in square Pillars of that Order, that hath been yet executed in or about Bath". It is certainly a well-balanced and fashionable design that must have delighted its owner. Belcombe Court is the best-preserved of the three villas that Wood designed on sites around the fringes of Bath; Lilliput Castle (1738), a small lodge-like building, is now incorporated in a larger house; Titanbarrow, near Bathford

70. *Belcombe Court, Bradford-on-Avon (John Wood the Elder, 1734) (© Crown copyright, N.M.R.)*

(1748), was designed as a somewhat richer version of Belcombe Court in the Corinthian order but its appearance has been much affected by later changes. None of these resembled the more Italian-influenced villa, as it developed in the hands of Campbell or Kent, for example. However, after Belcombe Court, Wood would be turning all his attention to a far greater house-building venture in Bath that would be much more in the grand Palladian style.

10 The Revival Continues – John Wood in Bath

John Wood had already built, on the north side of Queen Square, a row of houses masquerading as a palace. He would soon have an opportunity to design a real one. In 1728, Ralph Allen's bid to supply stone from his Combe Down quarries for part of Greenwich Hospital had been unsuccessful. The price and ease of supply were already competitive. He had achieved this by the positive support he had given to the creation of the Avon Navigation to Bristol (whence stone could be shipped to London) and by building a wharf, near the bottom of what is now called Prior Park Road, linked to the quarries by a railway line (which relied on a good braking system and horse-power to haul back the empty waggons). The thoroughness of his planning is further evidenced by the rows of cottages that he had built for his workmen, by John Wood, both near the quarries and near the wharf. The rejection of his bid had been on grounds of quality and Allen was piqued. He decided to kill two birds with one stone (to use an appropriate metaphor) by building a large mansion for himself on a site at the head of a steep-sided valley, next to his quarries, that would not only give him incomparable views of Bath but would allow the world to see the splendour of his building and, more importantly, the material in which it was built.[1]

Allen turned to Wood to produce a design that would not only match the quality of its siting but would rival any of the grand Palladian designs of its era. Pevsner calls it "the most ambitious and the most complete re-creation of Palladio's villas on English soil". It has to be said straightaway that what we see today is very different from Wood's original idea. Prior Park today might, in different circumstances, have been one of the greatest of English country houses but its history has been a series of misfortunes. Work began in 1734 but by 1738 the disagreements between the two men were so serious that Wood was dismissed, to be replaced by his Clerk of Works, Richard Jones, and Wood's design underwent many changes. After Allen's death, the contents and fittings were sold and the house neglected. After the buildings were acquired in 1830 for use as a catholic college, many alterations were made including the building of a church on the west side and the building of a huge stairway (designed by H.E.Goodridge) in front of the main block. The buildings were gutted by fire in 1836 and again in 1990. The buildings are now used as a school but divorced from the grounds. These, after many years of neglect, have been partly restored by the National Trust (who opened them to the public in 1995) but their severance from the former house is all too evident.

1. As a result of this campaign, part of St.Bartholomew's Hospital was built in Bath stone but its critics' fears were justified and later had to undergo substantial repair through the stone's inability to withstand the corrosive effect of London's smokey atmosphere.

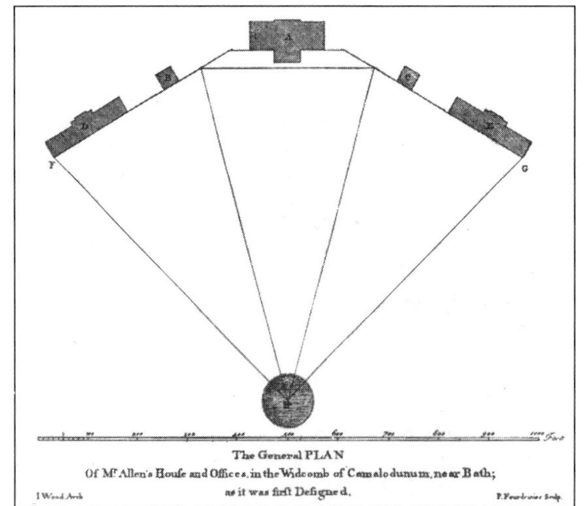

71. *Planned layout of Prior Park, Bath: from John Wood the Elder's* An Essay Towards a Description of Bath

However, the main elements of Wood's design are still there or are, at least, easy enough to visualise. He planned five buildings along three sides of a dodecagon, giving a sweep to the composition exactly matching the sweep of the head of the valley (fig.71). The general concept of a main block with elongated wings fitted the idea behind many of Palladio's villas. The design of the central block was clearly based on Campbell's first published (but unexecuted) design for Wanstead House, Essex ('Wanstead I' – see fig.72). This had been Campbell's largest house (it was demolished in 1822) and his most visited. Allen wished to surpass it in scale and grandeur. The main block of Prior Park had only 15 bays against the 21 of Wanstead II (the executed version) but Wood's east and west wings were each of 17 bays and between each wing and the main block was to stand an elegant square pavilion serving as a *porte-cochère* for

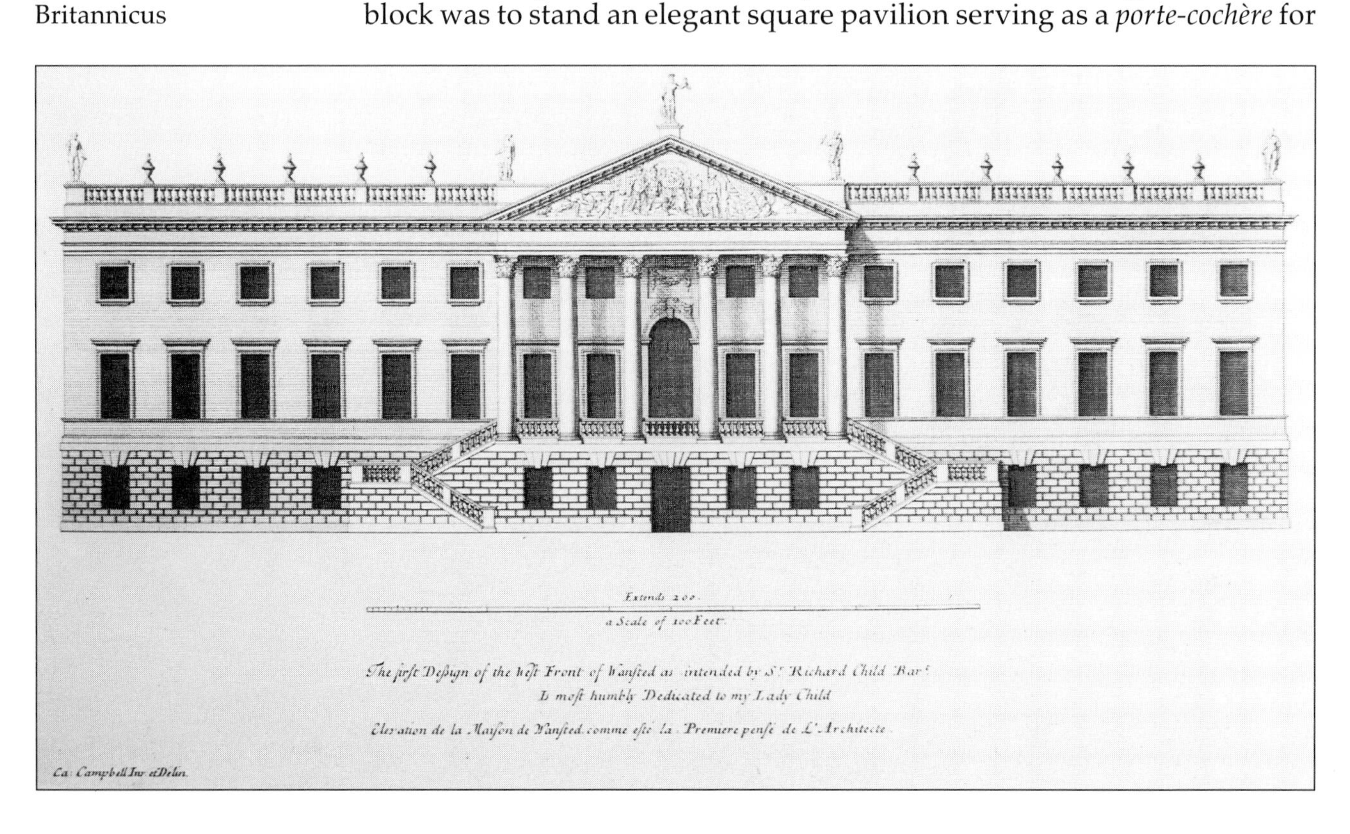

72. *Wanstead I: unexecuted design by Colen Campbell, published in* Vitruvius Britannicus

73. *Prior Park, Bath: drawing by W.Wills after Thomas Hearne (1785), incorrectly showing 13 bays in the main house. (© Crown copyright, N.M.R.)*

coaches to stop under. Two contemporary engravings (figs.73 & 74) give an idea of the final version, in which the pavilions have been joined to the wings and connected to the main block by covered arcaded passages. The engravings also indicate the importance of the grounds to which Allen devoted so much attention during the remainder of his life, using the services of Alexander Pope (well known at the time for the gardens and grottos he had designed for himelf in Twickenham) and, later, Lancelot ('Capability') Brown. In 1755, a Palladian Bridge was built at the lower end

74. *Prior Park, Bath and Ralph Allen's railway in 1750: from an engraving by Anthony Walker*

of the plunging valley in imitation of the one at Wilton. The design is identical except that the central pillars in the arcade are spaced more widely apart than the others and the interior surfaces of the building have less enrichment. So fate did not treat John Wood kindly here. Let us look at his next major project.

Anyone arriving at Bath railway station to visit the city for the first time may wonder if they are in the right place. The curved classical façades at the corner of Manvers Street, opposite the station, offer some encouragement but this is quickly dispelled as the visitor proceeds up Manvers Street itself. At last, as the street becomes Pierrepont Street, some rather bleak Georgian terraces appear on the right-hand side and, on the left, a glimpse through a columned opening reveals some slightly richer examples of 18th-century buildings. Ahead, looms the intimidating bulk of the Empire Hotel. Later, as Bath's glorious hillside terraces unfold and the beauty of Bathwick is revealed, the visitor may begin to wonder why, in Bath's heyday, more was not made of the level areas south of the Abbey enfolded by the sweep of the river Avon (the 'Ham') and why the little that does exist is so uninspiring. It was not for want of trying so far as John Wood was concerned. He first envisaged a 'Circus' on the northern part of the Ham but it was never built. We have also seen how his enthusiastic vision for 'Troy Novant' included a Royal Forum. This would have been a vast double piazza, straddling the river, and would, as the name implies, have been the town centre, the main focal point of the life of the community. The idea had, at first, been dismissed by the City Council as "chimerical" and Wood himself recognised that the low-lying boggy state of the land would make building difficult, not least for the construction of the necessary crossing of the river. So in 1739 he presented a reduced scheme limited to what we see today – North Parade, South Parade, Pierrepont Street and Duke Street, all supported by an arcaded terrace – and began work in 1740. In the layout of the area shown in his *Essay* (fig.75), he still optimistically indicates the site of the Royal Forum but, of course, it was never to be.

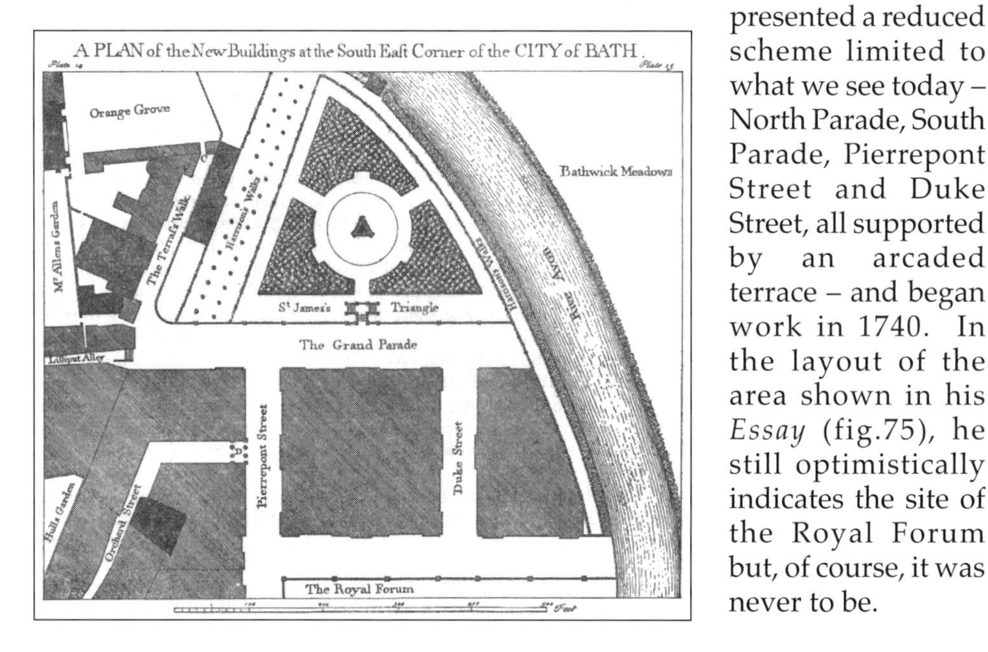

75. *The Parades, Bath: layout plan from John Wood the Elder's* An Essay Towards a Description of Bath

The reason is probably to be found in Wood's account of the work in his *Essay*. The north and south facing fronts of the central block of the development (i.e. facing North and South Parades) were to be given, like Queen Square, a temple front and a lavish display of Corinthian columns and pilasters with all the other enrichments that the Corinthian order required. But, Wood reports,

76. Duke Street, Bath, with scarcely a glazing bar to be seen (John Wood the Elder, 1740)

> a Scheme, contrived by one of the Tenants, broke out, to lay aside the Ornaments; to alter the Proportion of the Walk; and to erect the Terrass Wall with Rubble Stone, so as to have no reference to the building above.

Now Tim Mowl and Brian Earnshaw have little doubt that the hand behind this 'Scheme' was that of Ralph Allen, who had taken leases on five of the houses, purely, no doubt, as a financial investment. The loss of the 'Ornaments' had a radical effect on the prestige and character of this part of town and, thereby, on the course its future development would take. "Moving for an easy profit," say Mowl and Earnshaw, "Allen ensured that fashionable Bath would rise northwards up the hill on steep, difficult, building sites, not southwards and near the centres of entertainment. When Ralph Allen's philanthropy is being honoured, this action should be remembered." Because this corner of Georgian Bath has remained on the fringe of the town centre, it has been more vulnerable to insensitive alterations than the more prestigious parts. Writing in 1980, Ison lists some of the problems:

> Modern shop fronts have been inserted into some houses, and the proportions of many windows have been spoilt by cutting down the aprons, splaying reveals, and removing the sash-bars. Parapets have been cut away, terminal vases removed, and the central feature of the east side of Pierrepoint Street was refaced in bad taste.

He complains of the substitution of iron railings for balustrades and of standard lamps for obelisks and of many internal changes spoiling the clarity of the original arrangements. The situation has probably got rather worse since then, certainly in Pierrepont Street. Thus it is that our visitor's first

77. *Mineral Water Hospital, Upper Borough Walls, Bath (John Wood the Elder, 1738-42)*

encounter with the work of John Wood will be a disappointment. However, Duke Street, tucked away in the middle of it all, remains wholly residential and gives a flavour of how this corner of Bath might once have been (fig.76); another feature that remains characterful is the pillared opening on the west side of Pierrepont Street known as St.James's Portico. In all this, let it not be overlooked that John Wood was remaining every bit as true to the Palladian principles of design as he had been at Queen Square.

Wood's other design project at about this time was also not without its difficulties. A proposal for a Mineral Water Hospital had been put forward in 1716 by Lady Elizabeth Hastings and Henry Hoare (soon to be the creator of Stourhead). They could see that people were flocking to Bath for the water treatments (or merely to be fashionable) but that there were many more with, perhaps, a greater need, who could not afford to come. The idea was quickly supported and Beau Nash, Dr.William Oliver, Ralph Allen and John Wood himself became benefactors and active supporters. Allen donated the stone from his quarry and Wood his architectural services. (A cynic might suggest that what partly motivated these philanthropists was the thought that a specific venue for the lower classes, where their activities in Bath could be controlled, was better for the city's fashionable image than a free-for-all.) There were many delays and even an enforced change to the site but, eventually, work started on a site in Upper Borough Walls in 1738 and was completed in 1742. In his *Essay*, Wood confesses that the "real plan" to which he worked was not the one that had been put about to seek public support and funds. The building as we see it today (and now called the Royal National Hospital for Rheumatic Diseases – fig.77) carries a large extra storey, added in 1793 to the design of John Palmer, and an extension built in 1858 to the design of Manners and Gill. All this, and the cramped and busy location, tend to shout down Wood's original design which, if not one of his greatest, would, at the time, have been another stately contribution to Bath's growing array of buildings in a restrained Palladian style.

The main north-facing façade is of 11 bays with a temple front having four engaged unfluted Ionic columns. The doorway has a pediment, echoing the major one above, but the windows have plain surrounds. The building has since been given a semi-Victorian air by the style of the lettering below the pediment, spelling out the (original) name of the institution, and by a Victorian royal coat of arms in the tympanum of the pediment. It was here that Wood had planned a bas-relief representing the Good Samaritan; it was never implemented but the idea was borrowed for the later extension (built in a style intended to be sympathetic to the original building). Another detail in Wood's design that was omitted was a pair of human figures resting on the pediment of the doorway. This is a shame as it would have been a rare example in England of this Palladian motif (as previously discussed in relation to Wilton House).

The Hospital treated up to 150 patients who were all non-residents of Bath. They would only be admitted if they came with three shillings supplied by their own parishes to cover either the cost of their return or the cost of their burial. Until 1830, when pipes were laid to the King's Bath, patients had to walk to one of the Baths or be carried.

Although John Wood's dream of a Royal Forum was not to be realised, his vision of a Grand Circus "for the Exhibition of Sports" remained undimmed. This might seem an even less likely candidate to get off the ground than the Forum but, remarkably, it was the one that was realised. Not that 'Sports' were to feature in the development; indeed it is not clear what they might have ever amounted to (though cricket enthusists might feel that Bath's Circus would have made a charming ground for the game that was to become so popular later in the 18th century). But first Gay Street, that links Queen Square with The Circus (or 'King's Circus' to give it its original name), needs a mention. The length on the east side, between Old King Street and George Street was built by the elder Wood between 1735 and 1740. (The rest was completed, in the same style, by Wood the Younger after 1754 as part of the Circus project in order to complete the link to the south.) Again the design is in John Wood's characteristic plain style which we have seen in all his terraces (bar the north side of Queen Square) and at St.John's Hospital. But here we are starting to climb the hills of Bath in a serious way; so, for the first time, Wood has to devise a system for fitting the houses

78. East side of Gay Street, Bath, including No.41 on the corner (John Wood the Elder, 1735-40)

to the rising ground. Each house is stepped above its southern neighbour. The problem for the designer in this situation is what to do about the projecting horizontal features (in this case, for example, a plat band and the cornice) which go right across the width of each house. Are they to be simply broken and given a return edge (as if the terrace had been snapped apart into its component houses) or should some device be found to allow one house façade to flow into the next? In Gay Street, Wood chose the first option but later Bath architects would use the second, with some considerable success.

How are we to explain the delightful anomaly in all this, of No.41 (fig.78), which sits prominently on the southern corner with Old King Street? It used to be thought that this had been built by John Wood for his own occupation[2] but Ison's research shows it to to have been built for Richard Marchant, a wealthy and influential Quaker (who was also the Woods' lawyer). Ison further maintains that, despite the plaque on the site to say that the younger Wood later lived there, there is no evidence at all to suggest that he did. It is a superbly rich composition, comprising a three-storeyed bow, with a cluster of three windows on each floor, that on the first floor forming a Venetian window with four pairs of engaged Ionic columns; the lively Gibbsian surrounds on the two lower floors are balanced higher up by a projecting band and cornice and by three prominent vases above the parapet, which constitute an essential part of the composition. Perhaps it was this radical departure from the norm that encouraged the first leaseholder of No.8, some years later, so to enrich the façade of his house that it became known as 'The Carved House'.

79. *The Circus, Bath: detail of the ground-floor frieze (John Wood the Elder, 1754)*

John Wood had contracted to buy the land for the upper part of Gay Street and The Circus at the end of 1753 but died just before it was formally conveyed in 1755. But he lived long enough to witness the laying of the foundation stone of one section of The Circus in 1754. So his son was left to execute it, but the concept and the design were the father's. The Circus is a curious mixture. At one level, there is a chirpiness about it that makes you smile. There are the little carved images in the ground floor frieze (where they can easily be seen just above eye level) inviting you to play the game of trying to spot two the same (fig.79). And then there are the acorns running

2. This prompted the catty remark from Pevsner, in the first (and to date only) edition of *North Somerset and Bristol* in the Buildings of England series: "Architects have a way of designing for themselves at a higher pitch than for clients".

***80**. Part of The Circus, Bath (John Wood the Elder, 1754)*

all the way round the top of the buildings drawing you away from the architecture into speculation about why they are there: are they a reference to Bladud and his pigs, perhaps, or to the Druids and their oak trees?[3] Above all there is the comic element of a space in which everything looks the same: is it you that is moving or are the buildings spinning around you? But the boldness of the concept and the cleverness of its execution is what you try and hold on to. The division of the circle into three rather than four equal parts (possibly based on a freely-interpreted plan of Stonehenge drawn by Inigo Jones) is what gives it its magic, that sense of enclosure as the circle is entered. This feeling of awe would have been greater when the central space was first laid out as an open paved area with just a water supply tank in the centre.[4] In contrast to The Parades, the architectural detail is so pronounced that one can safely assume that the younger John Wood was not forced into any compromises (fig.80). The Circus consists of three 3-storey blocks each of 35 bays and each bay is flanked by two, coupled, columns, making a grand total of 648 individual columns. Each column is unfluted and is engaged only to the extent of one quarter of its volume. Moreover, the elder Wood, as designer, was able to indulge himself with a different order for each of the three storeys, Roman Doric, Ionic and Corinthian, the last incorporating its correct extra adornment in the form of masks and garlands.[5] The façade is topped by a parapet which breaks forward over each pair of columns where it supports one of the afore-mentioned acorns. Neither doorways nor windows receive any elaboration of treatment which might compete with all the other strong features – indeed, the use of windows without any form of surround (or architrave) was, for Bath, a minor revolution. Above all, we have here a statement of Wood's personal vision deriving from a strange mix of semi-mythological beliefs. Its general form is without precedent yet, to the end, he has remained true to the language of Palladianism.

3. Bladud, the legendary founder of Bath (and a descendant of Brutus, founder of *Troy Novant*), while himself a leper and outcast from the English Royal court, discovered the healing powers of the hot springs while the scabrous pigs he was tending rooted for acorns; Stonehenge and other stone circles were partly the inspiration for The Circus.
4. Again, Pevsner is unkind, referring to the old plane trees (which fill the central space) "which are now so much more splendid than the buildings".
5. For a discussion on whether the orders were used correctly, see *John Wood, Architect of Obsession*.

11 Palladio Established

What attracts the majority of visitors to Stourhead, now a property of the National Trust, is not the House but its world famous gardens. These were created by Henry Hoare's second son, another Henry, who inherited the estate when his father died in 1725, though he did not become entitled to possession until 1741 when his mother died. Henry Hoare II was known to later generations of the family as 'The Magnificent' to distinguish him from his father, known as 'The Good'. (We have seen an example of his good deeds in Bath; his memorial in Stourton church refers to many more.) Prior to his mother's death, he at first spent his time between London and a hunting lodge at Quarley on the family's land there but, in 1734, he bought Wilbury Manor from his uncle, William Benson. He went on the Grand Tour in 1738 but returned in 1741 when his mother died. His desire to immerse himself in the creation of the gardens may have sprung first from the death of his wife in 1743 and later that of his son and heir in 1751.

He began his work on the grounds in earnest in 1744. By this date, the formal style of garden layout with parterres and straight avenues had disappeared in favour of a more 'natural' approach, using and enhancing the attributes of the countryside itself. The best known proponent of 'landscape gardening' was 'Capability' Brown, who would be engaged at Corsham Court and at Bowood House in Wiltshire, but the layout of the grounds at Stourhead were undertaken by Henry Hoare himself. He sought to create not merely fine vistas, to which the hilly terrain lent itself, but various circuits within his estate that his family and visitors could enjoy either on foot or by carriage. For the buildings, he employed as architect Henry Flitcroft (1697-1769), to whom he remained loyal throughout his life. This is 'Burlington' Harry, a nickname indicating that he was a protégé of Lord Burlington and, indeed, we have already encountered him as Burlington's executant architect at Tottenham House. His father had been a labourer in the gardens at Hampton Court and had managed to get Henry apprenticed into the carpentry trade. His later rise to greater things is attributed to his falling off some scaffolding while working at Chiswick House and breaking his leg. Lord Burlington was concerned for the young man's welfare and, while visiting him on one occasion in his sick-bed, observed him drawing and, impressed by his skill, engaged him as an assistant architect. Hence the nickname and Flitcroft's dedication to the Burlington credo. Through Burlington's influence, he was appointed to a number of important Clerkships of the Works during the 1720s which established his career. He is best known, perhaps, for his work at Woburn Abbey, Bedfordshire and for the colossal house of Wentworth Woodhouse in Yorkshire. Early work for Hoare included an alteration to the house (not reproduced after the 1902 fire), a house at Clapham Common, a 'Venetian seat' at Stourhead (now gone) and the Temple of Ceres (later re-dedicated to Flora). These last two items were part of Hoare's original circuit around his grounds but he soon began to fulfil his ambition for a grander one in the valley below the house.

When the Temple of Ceres was built, in 1745, it overlooked a small rectangular basin and spring; beyond lay a stream and some ponds. All this was turned into the lake we see today by the formation of a dam. With Flitcroft's buildings as punctuation marks, Hoare would, over a period of about 20 years, create not merely some delightful gardens but what was, in effect, a theme park for discerning visitors. The theme was Virgilian, that of the wanderings of Aeneas and the founding of Rome. The Temple of Ceres (Flora), for example, has the inscription over the door 'Procul, O procul este profani!' ('Begone, you who are uninitiated, begone!'), the words Sybil spoke to Aeneas when about to lead him into the underworld and reveal the future history of Rome. The Grotto, later on the circuit, represented the underworld itself. The passage downwards is gentle ('facilis descensus Averno') but, as Sybil had warned, it is the ascent, the leaving, that is much harder – thus the steep steps at the other end. In the Grotto itself, there is first the figure of a sleeping nymph, another allusion to Aeneas's travels, and, in the final cave, the figure of the River God (sculpted by John Cheere) who points in the direction of the Pantheon, or Temple of Hercules. This is a reference to the advice given to Aeneas by Tiber to seek the Arcadian king whom he finds worshipping at an altar dedicated to Hercules. (Not a lot of people know that – but many did in the 18th century!) And people flocked to see it, as they do today. In 1776, Mrs Lybbe Powys recorded in her diary that the village inn was full and, in nearby Mere, the last available room had been taken by Horace Walpole and Robert Adam. One regular visitor was Coplestone Warre Bampfylde, a particular friend of Hoare. He was an amateur artist and a number of his drawings exist that help us to see how the gardens appeared in Hoare's time. He was also an amateur landscape gardener and architect, and created lakes and a garden at his own estate at Hestercombe, on the southern edge of the Quantock Hills in Somerset, which are currently being restored (2000). Apart from a Tuscan-style temple, there is an interesting tribute to his friendship with Hoare in the form of an inscribed classical urn.

The garden and its buildings at Stourhead must be seen as one with the house. As Gervase Jackson-Stops explained,

> The same restrained architecture, based on antique precedents and harmonic proportions, can be found indoors as well as out: in the perfect cube of Campbell's entrance hall as in the perfect circle of Flitcroft's Pantheon. The same idealized views of classical landscape, after Claude and Poussin, hanging on the walls of Colt Hoare's picture gallery, can be brought to life on the walk encircling the lake. The same poets and philosophers whose works crowd the bookshelves of his

library are behind the literary references and inscriptions found throughout his grandfather's garden.[1]

Richard Colt Hoare, who became Henry Hoare II's heir, was the son of his daughter Anne. Henry's elder daughter, Susanna, was married (after her first husband had died) to Thomas Bruce of Tottenham, Ist Earl of Ailesbury.[2] It was his father who had married Lord Burlington's sister. Thus a formidable Palladian network developed in Wiltshire involving Burlington, Flitcroft, Charles Bruce, Thomas Bruce, Henry Hoare I, Henry Hoare II and William Benson, and the triangle of Stourhead, Tottenham and Wilbury. For good measure, Henry Hoare II was, for a time, MP for Salisbury and was also a regular visitor to Amesbury Abbey, the former home of his uncle William Benson and later the Palladian setting in which the Duchess of Queensbury played hostess to a fashionable artistic set.

***81**. Temple of Flora, Stourhead (Henry Flitcroft, 1745)*

So to the buildings themselves. The Temple of Flora (1745) (fig.81) is a small Roman-style temple with four Doric columns supporting a pediment. The alternating garlanded ox skulls (*bucrania*) and rosettes (or *paterae*) in the frieze are a common Roman/ Palladian style of decoration. The room beyond, no doubt used for resting or refreshment, contains a niche in the rear and side walls with urns and statues. It is in a tiny building like this that it is, perhaps, easier to understand the attraction of Roman architecture to people like Hoare and his friends than in grander creations. Its simplicity gives it an aura of timeless charm but it only succeeds through the accuracy of its design and the perfection of its craftsmanship. It is a narrow line between classical perfection and crude pastiche.

1. See his fine essay on Stourhead in *The Country House in Perspective*.
2. His uncle, whom he succeeded, had been 3rd Earl of Ailesbury but on his death an earldom was created by special limitation to the barony of Bruce. Thus Thomas is confusingly referred to as the 1st Earl although his uncle was the 3rd Earl.

82. *The Pantheon, Stourhead (Henry Flitcroft, 1753)*

The Pantheon (1753) (fig.82) is almost Stourhead's trademark appearing in virtually every painting or photograph intended to convey a 'general view' of the gardens. This is a tribute to Hoare who clearly chose its siting with great care. The building itself is a striking composition with a hexastyle Corinthian portico *in antis* flanked by astylar bays each with a pedimented niche in its lower half containing a statue – both to the front and to the side – and, inside, a large niche and urn. Pevsner makes the point that these bays screen the junction between the portico and the rotunda more successfully than in the original building in Rome (a weakness that is regularly remarked upon). Beyond the portico is an anteroom leading into the rotunda. A Pantheon indeed with seven statues of deities each set on a great block of marble-veneered stone within a large niche rising from the floor. The most striking is that of Hercules himself by Michael Rysbrack. Each niche is surmounted by a carved panel and the whole by a carved frieze (more *bucrania*) and the coffered domed ceiling rising above.

Many visitors do not trouble to visit the Temple of Apollo (1765) (fig.83) because it can be seen from several points in the grounds (if not as clearly as in Hoare's day) and a stiff climb is required to reach it. But, apart from the rewarding view, this temple is the most exciting of the three and deserves closer inspection. (There are also further tastes of the 18th-century theme park experience as you cross the road through a rising and twisting rocky set of steps and leave by a dark 'tunnel of love' which goes under it.) The reference to Apollo is still Virgilian but, this time, Flitcroft has been influenced by a more exotic Roman precedent, the Temple of the Sun at Baalbek in Syria

83. Temple of Apollo, Stourhead (Henry Flitcroft, 1765)

discovered and recorded by Robert Wood in 1751 but not published until 1757. There are three plates in his *Ruins of Balbec* which show the ruins as he found them (fig.84) and Flitcroft's own free interpretation is imaginative and impressive.[3] The centre of the structure is a simple cylinder, on a raised circular platform, divided into 12 bays each with a niche for a statue (except one where there is a door) and a roundel above. At the top there are four equally spaced thermal windows. The roof originally had a saucer dome (like the Pantheon) but was later given more drama by being raised to its present proportions. But the greater drama comes from the surrounding circular arcade of twelve Corinthian columns because its entablature is not itself circular but is a circle with twelve bites, or scallops, taken out of it, creating a continuous swinging movement all around the building. This sounds as if the general effect should be Baroque yet, curiously, it is not. It is more like a gentleman of discreet elegance who has chosen to wear a jauntier necktie than usual rather than one seeking to dress outrageously. The Temple is, of course, nothing more than an exquisite and very expensive folly. But it is an interesting indication of how the classical vocabulary in Georgian Britain had moved on, something to be explored in the next chapter. And in the same year, Flitcroft even tried his hand at a form of Gothic, building Alfred's Tower for Hoare, that imposing three-sided structure, 160 feet high, that can be seen from miles around on its prominent site to the north-west of the house and gardens. The Tower formed part of an outer Stourhead circuit that visitors could enjoy on horseback or in their carriages. Yet the theme of Aeneas is not entirely discarded as his great-grandson Brutus was the legendary founder of the English line of kings of whom Alfred was the greatest.

3. Sir William Chambers' Temple of the Sun at Kew is probably a more accurate interpretation of the original at Baalbek but is more boring than Flitcroft's.

As a relief from this intellectual approach to garden planning, it is worth jumping back, just 50 years or so before Stourhead gardens were planned, to Wilton, as it was before the 9th Earl of Pembroke introduced *his* changes. Celia Fiennes, the traveller and diarist who lived at Newton Toney in the days before William Benson built Wilbury Manor, made a visit to Wilton at the end of the 17th century and described the gardens in breathless detail:

84. Temple of the Sun, Baalbek, Syria: engraving from Ruins of Balbec *by Robert Wood (1757). (British Architectural Library, R.I.B.A., London)*

> The Gardens are very fine, with many gravel walkes with grass squaires set with fine brass and stone statues, with fish ponds, and basons with figures in the middle spouting out water, dwarfe trees of all sorts and a fine flower garden, much walle fruite: the river runns through the garden that easeily conveys by pipes water to all parts. Grottoe is at the end of the garden just the middle off the house, its garnished with many fine figures of the Goddesses, and about 2 yards off the doore is severall pipes in a line that with a sluce spouts water up to wett the Strangers; in the middle roome is a round table, a large pipe in the midst, on which they put a crown or a gun or a branch,and so it spouts the water through the carvings and poyntes all around the room at the Artists pleasure to wet the Company; there are figures at each corner of the roome that can weep water on the beholders, and by a straight pipe on the table they force up the water into the hollow carving of the rooff like a crown or coronet to appearance, but is hollow within to retaine the water forced into it in great quantityes, that disperses in the hollow cavity

> over the roome and descends in a shower of raine all about the roome; on each side is two little roomes which by the turning their wires the water runnes in the rockes you see and hear it, and also it is so contrived in one room that it makes the melody of Nightingerlls and all sorts of birds which engaged the curiosity of the Strangers to go in and to see, but at the entrance of each room, is a line of pipes that appear not till by a sluce moved it washes the spectators, designed for diversion. The Grottoe is leaded on the top where are fish ponds, and just without the grottoe is a wooden bridge over the river, the barristers [balusters] are set out with Lyons set thick on either side with their mouths open and by a sluce spout out water each to other in a perfect arch the length of the bridge; there are fine woods beyond the house and a large parke walled in.[4]

Henry Hoare II, like his father before him, rubbed shoulders with the great and the good of Georgian society in his capacity as their banker and adviser. One such association that he no doubt came to regret was with the elder William Beckford of Fonthill, known better as Alderman Beckford through his membership of the Common Council of the City of London of which he was twice Lord Mayor; for on his death in 1770, Hoare found himself, together with his son-in-law, Lord Bruce, an executor of Beckford's will which was to cause him endless difficulties. Beckford had bought the Fonthill estate in 1745, with his vast wealth from dealings in the City and, more particularly, from his estates in the West Indies. It contained a sprawling mansion that had been given a 'modern' front earlier in the century. In 1755, it was destroyed in a fire and Beckford instantly ordered a new house to be built. To design and build it he chose a man called Hoare (no relation to the bankers) about whom so little is known that he is referred to as 'Mr Hoare'. He is variously described as a builder or bricklayer from London, though the Court House at Maidstone, Kent is attributed to him as an architect. However that may be, the design of his house at Fonthill, if not showing much originality (being a close copy of Colen Campbell's Houghton Hall, Norfolk but without its towers) was a grand Palladian composition (fig.85) that would have had no peer in Wiltshire until New Wardour Castle came along in 1771. No wonder it was known as 'Fonthill Splendens'. The interiors were not Palladian at all but reflected Beckford's taste for the Baroque. In particular, it contained a large gloomy space misleadingly known as the Egyptian Hall but which bore little resemblance to the design of that name in *I Quattro Libri* on which Lord Burlington had based his Assembly Rooms at York. So it is no surprise, as the younger William Beckford's mind became affected by his Gothic dream leading to the building of the notorious Fonthill Abbey, that, in 1807, Fonthill Splendens should be

4. *The Journal of Celia Fiennes* (Cresset, London, 1947).

85. Fonthill Splendens (Mr. Hoare, begun 1755, demolished 1807): engraving by J.Buckler. (© Crown copyright, N.M.R.)

demolished. Some of its rococo ironwork was re-used by James Wyatt to adorn the great central staircase at Dodington House, Gloucestershire.[5]

Fonthill Splendens was a sad loss, made sadder by the disasters that befell the Abbey and its eventual destruction, but there is one enigmatic feature of the estate that remains, and can be readily viewed as it stands close to the road between Wilton and Hindon. This is the archway at Fonthill Bishop (fig.86) which serves as an estate lodge divided into two by the archway itself. There is a long-standing tradition that it was designed by Inigo Jones.

86. Fonthill Archway (attributed to John Vardy, d.1765)

5. At No.206 Castle Street (Milford Hall Hotel), Salisbury, the main door has a portico with wooden columns carved in the form of palm trees; these are reputed to come from Fonthill Abbey but their style is far more suggestive of the oriental taste of Alderman Beckford shown in the interiors of Fonthill Splendens than the Gothic taste of his son.

For example, some auction sale particulars of 1829, in the Wiltshire and Swindon Record Office, state:

> The Lodge Entrance puts forth its claim for attention: it was designed by Inigo Jones: it is the oldest specimen of architecture upon the domain, and its simplicity and proportions display that classic taste with which the distinguished architect was so familiar.

There is certainly a boldness about it to make the attribution plausible; it could almost be one of his stage sets brought to life with its massive rustication and large grotesque faces in the keystones of the arch. Yet, unlike Bath Guildhall, for example, no explanation has ever been given as to why the King's architect should have supplied a design for this particular estate in Wiltshire. However, it is now believed (DoE) that it was built at about the same time as Fonthill Splendens and that the designer was John Vardy (d.1765), another protégé of Lord Burlington who took a special interest in the work of Inigo Jones.

87. Corsham Court: Picture Gallery, interior (Lancelot 'Capability' Brown, 1761-64). (Corsham Court Collection)

Another Wiltshire landowner at about this time who was anxious to display his promotion of the Palladian style was Paul Methuen who had acquired Corsham Court in 1745. He had been a leading clothier at Bradford-on-Avon but, unlike the Hoares, for example, or Francis Yerbury, abandoned his business life and took on that of the full-time country landowner. He first decided to extend his Elizabethan mansion on its north side and obtained designs from Nathaniel Ireson in 1747 and again in 1749. It was this later, Palladian, design that was executed but, as we are about to see, none of it remains. He was also anxious to display the fine collection of paintings that he had inherited from his cousin, the distinguished diplomat, Sir Paul Methuen. To create a picture gallery, as an eastern extension to the house, he decided to employ 'Capability' Brown, the landscape architect but who also practised as an architect, designing in the Palladian style.[6] Three other rooms in the house are Brown's work but the most memorable is the triple-cube picture gallery (1761-64) with its ceiling plasterwork by the Bristol stuccador, Thomas Stocking (fig.87). Its external appearance, which had always been very plain, was later gothicised by John Nash. As for the north range, this was first partly obliterated by Brown's work, was later replaced by a design of Nash and Humphry Repton and then this, in turn, was swept away by the 19th-century Elizabethan work of Thomas Bellamy.

In 1752, the Town Council of Devizes had built for the town the New Hall, or the Cheese Market as it often called (fig.88), designed by a man

88. New Hall, Devizes (Mr.Lawrence, 1752)

6. The restyling of Broadlands House, Hampshire for the 2nd Viscount Palmerston, is, perhaps, his best-known work.

89. Monkton House, Chippenham (1757)

called Lawrence.[7] The hall contained space for a covered market at ground level though this has since been filled in to provide offices. The west front, looking down the main street, is a charming composition with a nice balance between the rusticated base, and the Ionic columnated first floor and richly carved pediment above. The corner pilasters are a good touch but the constraints of the site have forced the designer to use an 'incorrect' odd number of columns. But it is easy to see that three openings would have been too few and five too many if the height of the building was to be maintained.

An elegant example of a mansion in the Palladian style can be found in a public park in Chippenham – Monkton House (fig.89), now converted into flats, overlooking the crazy golf and pitch and putt courses in Monkton Park. Perhaps 'sub-Palladian' would be a better decription as, although it shows all the neatness and restraint of John Wood's plainer terraces, the ground floor is level with the ground and the windows are that little bit too large to be truly Palladian. The Ionic porch in front of the main door is a striking feature although its flat top appears as a large slab of entablature above the columns and gives the impression that it may have been made up from bits of recycled stone carving. The name of the architect or builder is not known.

7. Nothing more is known about him and it is simply a coincidence that the man who became the landlord of the The Bear Inn across the road in 1771 was also called Lawrence, being the father of the boy who would become Sir Thomas Lawrence the portrait painter.

12 New Influences and Palladian Survival – I

By the middle of the 1750s, the Palladian revival was beginning to run out of steam. Campbell had long since died (1727) and those who had championed the Palladian cause would now follow him – for example, Leoni in 1746, Kent in 1748, Morris in 1749, Pembroke in 1751 and Burlington himself in 1753. Meanwhile studies of the ancient world were being made that would expose people's minds to possibilities outside the confines of the English and Scottish Palladianism based principally on Vitruvius, Palladio and Jones. Works by Comte de Caylus (1752) and Johann Winckelmann (1755) proclaimed the superiority of Greek architecture over Roman while Giovanni Battista Piranesi's *Antichità Romane* (1748) gave the world a pictorial reconstruction (if in a somewhat exaggerated form) of ancient Rome and his *Della Magnificenza ed architettura dei Romani* (1761) championed the cause of Roman architecture against that of Greece.

The Englishman, Robert Wood, set out from Naples with a party of friends and eventually reached Syria (then under Ottoman rule) in 1751 where, to the bewilderment of the inhabitants, he studied and drew the ancient Roman buildings. It was an adventurous and hazardous journey and the publication first of *The Ruins of Palmyra* in 1753 and then *The Ruins of Balbec* in 1757 were much-awaited events. While he was in Athens, Wood had met "Mr Stewart and Mr Revet ... two English painters", who were on a similar venture in the world of ancient Greece. They were James Stuart and Nicholas Revett whose publication of *Antiquities of Athens* between 1762 and 1789 would be even more consequential. In 1757, at the conclusion of a long and thorough Grand Tour, Robert Adam crossed the Adriatic to visit Spolato (the present-day Split) in order to see and record the Palace of Diocletian which had been built between 300 and 306 AD, that is to say, a good deal later than buildings in and around Rome that had been studied during and after the Renaissance. In 1764 he published *The Ruins of the Palace of the Emperor Diocletian at Spolatro* [as Adam insisted on calling it] *in Dalmatia*. The growing taste for classical designs was fed by the publication in 1766-7 of four volumes entitled *Collection of Etruscan, Greek and Roman Antiquities from the Cabinet of the Honourable William Hamilton* (the antiquarian and collector, Sir William Hamilton, British Ambassador in Naples). These would be of great value to Josiah Wedgwood and to many painters and sculptors. These are only the highlights of the proliferation at this time, both in volume and variety, of the publication of illustrated books with an architectural or design theme. Meanwhile, excavations at Pompeii and Herculaneum had begun and yet a different style of Roman art and architecture would gradually be revealed. Moreover, France, which had developed its own classical tradition in the 17th century but had been briefly outshone by English Palladianism, would once again assume a more central role in the development of neo-classicism.

A few words about the term 'neo-classicism', as used in architecture, might be timely here. It is obviously something to do with a style of architecture based on the 'classical' world of Greece and Rome. But (apart from the different ways the word is spelt and punctuated) it is not always clear whether it is being used (a) as an all-embracing term for all classical revivalism, including Renaissance and neo-Palladian architecture, or (b) as a term for a separate category of classical architecture in contradistinction to that of the Renaissance or to neo-Palladianism. The second approach would be to use the term in a rather artificial sense because were not Alberti, Serlio, Palladio and so on all neo-classicists? Are the neo-Palladians to be excluded merely because their inspiration came mainly from Palladio and Inigo Jones? The approach that causes the least difficulty is to use the term in the sense of an architecture based on archaeological precedent. Worsley deals helpfully with the matter in this way:

> ... neo-Classicism is an attitude towards the architecture of antiquity which can be present at any time. It is dangerous to use it to describe a period of architecture or indeed a style. Neo-Classicism was a feature of English architecture from the time of Inigo Jones and was particularly strong among amateur architects in the first half of the eighteenth century. In the second half of the century interest in neo-Classicism became more pervasive, especially among professional architects, but it was neither novel, nor was it all-embracing. Indeed it would be fair to argue that neo-Palladianism would be the dominant force in English architecture into the 1780s, despite the increasing importance of neo-Classicism.

The correctness of this last observation will certainly be borne out so far as the buildings of Wiltshire and Bath are concerned. In Bath, especially, the fabric of this growing city was so dominated by the Palladian style, which had been established from as early as the 1720s, that too novel a departure would have been regarded as unacceptable. John Wood the Younger, in particular, whilst developing his own style, would pay due respect to the inheritance that his father had left to Bath. Pulteney Bridge (begun in 1769) would be the first departure from the Palladian norm and there would not be another, and then only a modest departure, until the rebuilding of the Guildhall (begun in 1775). Even after that, the Bath architects were, during the 18th century, at any rate, readier to adopt Gothick than they were to depart from the Bath Palladian style of classicism. In Wiltshire, there would be examples of neo-classicism from 1759 (or even a little before). All these will be looked at in the next chapter when the Temple of Apollo (1765), that late work by Flitcroft at Stourhead, will be looked at again in the context of the new influences and changing taste.

In earlier chapters, John Wood the Younger has only been seen in his father's shadow, acting as his assistant or finishing off what his father had begun. He would now inherit, not only his father's practice, but his role as Bath's leading architect. He had come into his father's practice at an early age and in 1749 his father apparently had enough confidence in his abilities to leave him to superintend work at Liverpool's Exchange which the elder Wood had designed for the city. It would also appear that their employers treated them on equal terms because, later that year, both of them would be admitted as freemen of the city of Liverpool. But an honour bestowed upon the younger Wood alone was election as a member of Liverpool's 'Ugly Face Clubbe'. The citation of his credentials read as follows:

> A stone colour'd complexion, a dimple in his Attic Story. The Pillasters of his face fluted. Tortoise-ey'd, a prominent nose. Wild grin, and face altogether resembling a badger, and fine tho' smaller than Sir Christopher Wren or Inigo Jones's.

It is not known which he regarded as the greater honour. While the elder Wood was a man of vision and boldness, his son was equally energetic and was, perhaps, the more accomplished architect. There is a great deal of important work to come, not only in Bath, but at Standlynch, at Salisbury and at Hardenhuish (near Chippenham).

His first major task, after his father's death, was to complete the building of the King's Circus and Gay Street. He would then be free to develop Brock Street and the Royal Crescent. Other buildings put up at this period are also consistent with the fine architectural pedigree that had evolved in Bath. One is King Edward's Grammar School in Broad Street (1752) designed by the Bath architect and builder Thomas Jelly (d.1781) (fig.90). It is a

90. *King Edward's Grammar School, Broad Street, Bath (Thomas Jelly, 1752)*

delightful Palladian design of five bays, the central three slightly brought forward and pedimented. All nine windows have distinct surrounds and the lower four each have a segmental pediment. The pedimented door surround with Ionic engaged columns and pilasters would be a little too strong for the arrangement were it not for the energetic carving of the City Arms in the pediment that gives the necessary balance. The modillioned cornice and pediment surround and the balustrading over the outer bays give the whole composition great presence – as if it were on centre stage commanding the attention of the audience. The delight of encountering this building in the cramped and hectic (ironically-named) Broad Street is increased by the rarity in Bath of a building of this modest width and its contrast with the standard terraced format. The way it is set back from the street is also a rarity. According to Ison, the pillars with their shapely urns are "nearly contemporary" but the stone balustrades are modern and replace an original iron railing.

More consistent with the Bath domestic character are Bladud Buildings, the first development to take place along London Road, in 1755. London Road, as we now see it in its fully developed state, exudes the spirit of 18th-century Bath better, perhaps, than any other street, with its sinuous curve, its raised pavements and iron railings and its unremitting restraint and elegance. Unfortunately, Bladud Buildings, being the first section to be built and the nearest to the town centre, has lost many of its ground-floor rooms to shop use and it takes more of an effort to study it. In fact, the general design, which is either by Thomas Jelly or Thomas Atwood, is broadly in the Wood tradition although the first-floor windows in particular are rather taller than Wood ever used. The Buildings consist of 15 units each of three bays, the centre of each unit marked by a pediment over the first-floor window and the centre of the whole marked by a pediment over the three central bays. Two bays of No.6 have been

91. *Bladud Buildings, London Road, Bath (Thomas Jelly or Thomas Atwood, 1755): north pavilion*

altered to form a semi-circular bay which might have been a fine feature if it had been balanced by another one. The end units project slightly to form pavilions. That on the north end, away from the commercial mayhem, is a pleasing composition (fig.91). It is often said of Bladud Buildings that it is unique amongst the terraces for having been designed 'architecturally' at the rear as well as the front. The architect's best intentions have inevitably been compromised by later rear extensions but a comparison with the Royal Crescent, say, will show that at least he tried.

And it is to John Wood the Younger's Bath masterpiece that we should now turn. His first task was to develop the land he had acquired for the building of Brock Street (named after Wood's brother-in-law and building partner, Thomas Brock) which would serve as the link between the King's Circus and the Royal Crescent. These were clearly intended to be the great showpieces of Bath, to be a source of wonder, so Brock Street would need to be less dramatic. It was not begun until 1764, after the Circus/Gay Street development was complete, and some of its houses were still being built after the Royal Crescent was begun. This was always likely to lead to some variation in the street and there have been many alterations to it since. Nevertheless, it can be said that the standard outward appearance of the units is something new for Bath. The pedimented Doric or Ionic door cases (or, in some cases, porticos) are as John Wood the Elder might have designed them but the windows are arranged in clusters of three, many of them on the first floor in the form of a Venetian window, and have only a plain, projecting cill. In other words, as in the Circus, they have no surrounds (or architraves) but here, set in a plain, ashlared façade, their own plainness is more apparent (fig.92). It is a device that would henceforth become predominant in Bath.

92. *House in Brock Street, Bath (John Wood the Younger, 1764)*

93. Royal Crescent, Bath (John Wood the Younger, 1767)

The land for the Royal Crescent was acquired by Wood and Brock in 1766 and building work began the following year. For all its splendour and importance, The Royal Crescent was just the latest in a growing line of speculative housing developments in Bath. It consisted of 30 houses which would not only be occupied separately but actually be built separately, under the normal Bath system of sub-leases giving control over the design of the façades to Wood and Brock as head lessees. The first house to be built was No.1 (now a museum operated by the Bath Preservation Trust) for Brock's own occupation and, no doubt, it served as a model for the rest. It is the only house in which the windows have been restored to their original size and shape and with the original style of glazing bars. Any sense of the rhythmic perfection that the Royal Crescent must once have had has been lost as the details have been changed over the years. But it still has an impressive dignity and, of course, it is a building of special importance as the first arc-shaped terrace in Britain which would soon be an inspiration for many more. Its shape is closer to that of a third of a circle rather than a semi-circle; in other words, it is like one section of the Circus, more than doubled in length, and slightly bent in at the ends.

The treatment of the façade (fig.93), so very different from the Circus, which, by comparison, begins to look naive, is impeccably Palladian or, at any rate, Jonesian, as it could almost be Lindsey House in Lincoln's Inn

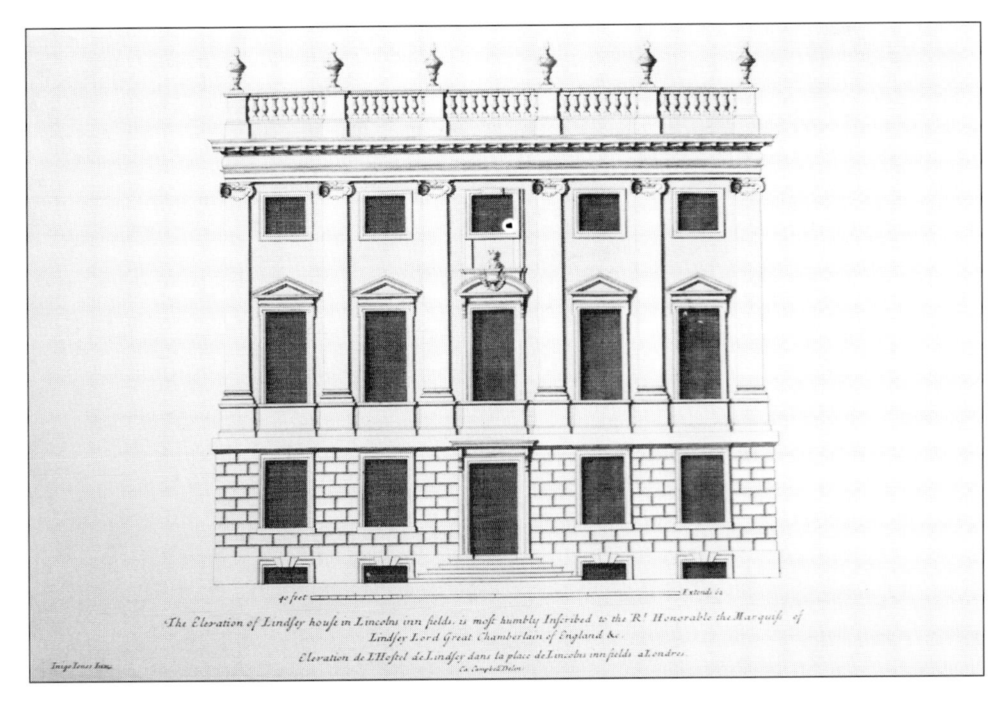

94. *Lindsey House, Lincoln's Inn Fields, London (attributed to Inigo Jones, 1640): engraving from* Vitruvius Britannicus.

Fields, attributed to Inigo Jones, in a curved and much-extended form (fig.94). The way Wood has used the giant Ionic order, however, (with plump, three-quarter, engaged columns) meets the needs of the vast length of the building better than the pilasters that were used for Lindsey House. The prominence of the columns then become a justification for the plain window openings (which follow the pattern established at the Circus and Brock Street). It is a grand composition which Inigo Jones himself would surely have admired.

There is just the matter, though, of its central feature. All Wood has done to mark the centre is to substitute paired columns for single ones on each side of the central bay (as he has at the ends and corners of the colonnade) and to give the central first-floor window a curved top. This hardly seems worth doing and it is no wonder that it soon came in for criticism –

> the wretched attempt to make a centre to the Crescent where none is necessary is absurd and preposterous, in a high degree. The pairing of the pillars is too small a difference to be noted in so large a building.[1]

So what might Wood have had in mind? There is one strong possibility. The only precedent for a curved colonnade on this scale was in Rome where Bernini had designed the two great colonnades that embrace the piazza in front of St.Peter's. The span of each arc is, indeed, almost identical to that of the Royal Crescent. As a feature to enable the eye to pause as it swept round the great arc, Bernini introduced two pairs of columns in place of the

1. From *The Stranger's Assistant and Guide to Bath* for 1773.

***95**. St. James's Parade, Bath (Thomas Jelly and/or John Palmer, c.1768)*

two single ones in the centre. But this central bay announces itself more clearly than at Bath by taking a good step forward from the rest. In a busy colonnade, consisting of four rows of columns, this was a necessary ploy if the centre was to be distinctly marked. Perhaps Wood felt that the smoother rhythm of the Royal Crescent would not have lent itself to a similar device. A purist might say that it would have been better still to have let that rhythm remain completely unbroken. A resident might be glad of some variation to find the way home on a foggy night!

At around this time there would be a great outpouring of effort in the expansion of Bath.[2] Work on Milsom Street had already been started in 1762, in a style very similar to Bladud Buildings and in accordance with plans submitted by John Horton. The Octagon Chapel, by Timothy Lightoler,[3] was opened in 1767. Belmont was begun in 1768 and, possibly in the same year, the extension of the city in the south-west began, with a development centred on St.James's Parade. The north-eastward expansion, along the London Road, was continued in 1769 with Paragon Buildings and Walcot Parade shortly after. It almost goes without saying that all of these are Palladian, St.James's Parade being the most eye-catching with a triple-window arrangement similar to Brock Street but with its first-floor Venetian windows given a stronger presence with a heavy continuous cornice and four stumpy supporting consoles (fig.95). Thomas Jelly was one of the developers but John Palmer (a name

2. The way Bath developed during Georgian times is tracked and illustrated in *The City of Bath* by Barry Cunliffe (Alan Sutton, Stroud, 1986).
3. Often rendered incorrectly as 'Thomas' (see Colvin).

96. Upper Assembly Rooms, Bath (John Wood the Younger, 1769)

that will appear more often later on) may also have been involved in the design. But it was the Circus that was proving to be the fashionable hub of Bath's development. Gay Street had been completed by 1761; by 1769 Brock Street was all but complete and the Royal Crescent had begun. In that year Wood was able to start work on what was arguably his most prestigious venture to date, the New, or Upper, Assembly Rooms[4] between Bennett Street and Alfred Street (whose own houses were not built till some years later).

For a building that would become the principal social centre of Bath society, the Assembly Rooms are curiously located being, one might say, 'nowhere in particular'. A newcomer to Bath will stumble over them by accident and not be able to find them again without a good map. So it comes as no surprise to find that the site originally selected was not this one, but on land to the north-west of Queen Square. After some disagreements about the development, Wood built a row of houses on it instead (Queen's Parade). In a competition for the design of the building to go on the alternative site, Wood's was preferred to one of Robert Adam which contained more architectural enrichment and would have been more costly. The cool elegance of Wood's design (fig.96) is certainly in the minimalist Palladian tradition with, perhaps, a nod in the direction of Greece; its massing brings to mind the Propylaea in Athens though the drama of the original would have been more effectively captured if it had been possible to turn the building to face down the hill.

4. The designations 'New' and 'Upper', now rarely used, were applied at a time when two older-established Assembly Rooms (Harrison's and Lindsey's) still existed on adjoining sites between the Abbey and North Parade.

97. *Tea Room, Upper Assembly Rooms, Bath (John Wood the Younger, 1769)*

Any richness is reserved for the interiors, especially the Ball Room (taking up the entire length of the northern block of the building) and the Tea Room (comprising about two-thirds of the southern block), with its less attenuated proportions and exquisite two-tier gallery (fig.97). The octagonal ante-room and Card Room are part of Wood's design but the rectangular room beyond was added in 1777 to the undistinguished design of an unknown architect. The Rooms were seriously damaged in the Second World War, the Ball Room being wholly destroyed, but they were ably restored by Sir Albert Richardson. They are the earliest set of buildings of Georgian Bath to be regularly open to the public and are a considerable asset to the town.

13 New Influences and Palladian Survival – II

It is only as we move into the 1760s and 1770s that, in Wiltshire at any rate, we begin to see the effect of the influences discussed in the last chapter. By now, all those early links with Lord Burlington and his circle lie in the past. But the tradition of excellence that had been established at the various country seats such as Wilton House, coupled with a great deal of wealth (both 'old' and 'new') and, in some cases, an urge to outdo one's neighbours, ensured that the leading architects of the day would continue to be represented in Wiltshire by their works. The first to be featured is, perhaps, the greatest of them all, Sir William Chambers (1723-1796). In his lifetime, he acquired a reputation for enormous learning, encyclopaedic knowledge of classical forms and, especially in his latter days as the Surveyor of the Works (when a great deal of his time was devoted to the building of Somerset House), for diligence and reliability (in complete contrast to James Wyatt who succeeded him). His great wisdom and experience was condensed into his *Treatise on Civil Architecture* (1759) which, for many years, was the chief resource of the serious architectural student. Horace Walpole called it "the most sensible book and the most exempt from prejudice that ever was written in that science". Thus Chambers was a worthy man on whom the bestowing of a knighthood would follow, one might think, as a matter of course. Yet, curiously, his knighthood was not a British honour at all, but Swedish. It was in 1770 that he was made a 'Knight of the Polar Star' and later the English king gave him permission to adopt the address of an English knight ("Chambers has Sir Williamized himself", wrote Walpole). Although Chambers had English parents and went to school in England, his father was a merchant in Gothenburg and William himself served with the Swedish East India Company from 1740 to 1749. However, he soon discovered that his principal interest was architecture and, in the course of his travels, he accumulated a large knowledge of Indian and Chinese architecture as well as European. He then began a serious study of architecture, first in Paris for a few months, and then, for five years, in Rome (where he had lodgings in the same building as Piranesi). Even as a student, he acquired a formidable reputation and Robert Adam, who was in Rome himself for part of this time, recognised Chambers as his superior, as a draughtsman, in his social contacts and with his air of wisdom. However, back in England, his career was slow to take off but he did publish *Designs for Chinese Buildings* in 1756 and, in 1757, was appointed tutor to the Prince of Wales, the future George III, who took a great interest in architecture.

It would have been while moving in such exalted circles, that Chambers met Lord Pembroke, the 10th Earl, who had inherited his father's interest in architecture and Chambers would spend "many long and happy hours" with

98. Triumphal Arch, Wilton House (Sir William Chambers, c.1758), (Wilton House Trust)

him. A number of projects for Wilton reached the drawing board; a bridge over the "Nadir" (Nadder), a Triumphal Arch in stone (to replace an earlier wooden one on the hill on the south side of the park) and a Roman temple (or *Casina*). It was these last two that would be executed, sometime in 1758 or 1759. A "Rocky Bridge" was also created by Chambers within the grounds but this no longer exists. (More substantial work by Chambers consisted of some interior re-shaping of the west wing of the house, including the creation of a library, but all this would disappear at the time of the more substantial alterations carried out by James Wyatt for the 11th Earl.) The purpose of the wooden arch had been to provide an eye-catcher on the southern skyline (to which the 9th Earl had aligned his Palladian Bridge) and also to support a magnificent lead copy of the statue of Marcus Aurelius on the Capitoline Hill which that great collector, the 8th Earl, had brought back from Rome. It is one thing to copy a Roman structure but it requires a virtuoso to design one of his own in a convincing and pleasing style and without recourse to any particular Roman precedent. Chambers' interpretation of the Roman triumphal arch (fig.98), with overtones of famous precedents like those of Septimius Severus, Constantine or Titus but not actually designed to look like like any of them, is a fine achievement. For over 40 years, it had remained a distant shape on the hillside but since about 1802, during the changes undertaken for the 11th Earl, the Arch has served as a formal entrance to Wilton House once the main approach had been switched from the east side to the north. That the Arch looks as if it had always been here is a tribute to the way Wyatt integrated it with two small pavilions which he added, one on either side.

The Casina at Wilton (fig.99) is superficially identical to Flitcroft's Temple of Flora (formerly Ceres) at Stourhead (fig.81) – the same Doric tetrastyle porch and the same frieze of alternating *bucrania* and *paterae*. But, first, a few minor differences will be observed (for example, the *bucrania* and the *paterae* have changed places and Chambers has added some unusually prominent mutules in the cornice and pediment) and, more significantly, the Casina has been designed to be seen from a distance and from below on the face of a steep slope – hence the rusticated basement and the balustrade above. This practical touch, to protect any visitor from falling off the porch, is, perhaps, some indication that, in earlier times, the building had some function apart from being a far object in the landscape and that all the exquisite workmanship that went into it was not undertaken in vain.

***99.** Casina, Wilton House (Sir William Chambers, c.1758). (Wilton House Trust)*

By 1760, Chambers' star was in the ascendant, helped by the accession of his 'pupil' George III. That year he designed the Gold State Coach (still the pride of the Royal Mews collection) and, in 1761, was made one of two Architects of the Works, Robert Adam being the other. Commissions poured in, including one (sometime in the 1770s) from the Duchess of Queensbury who wished to rebuild a decaying 'Chinese Temple' in the grounds of Amesbury Abbey.[1] Chambers' replacement (figs.100 & 101) itself required restoration in the 1980s. It is a quaint mixture of English Georgian building techniques and Chinese motifs. It is built in stone and timber with a great deal of decorative flint facing. The building may be outside the proper confines of this book, but it would be wrong to ignore the only surviving piece of chinoiserie attributed to Chambers outside Kew Gardens and a shame to miss the opportunity to include just one building in flint!

1. In the RCHM publication *Wilton House and English Palladianism*, it is suggested that another interpretation of correspondence between the Duchess and Chambers in 1772 is that Chambers was merely advising on the completion of a building begun many years before but left unfinished.

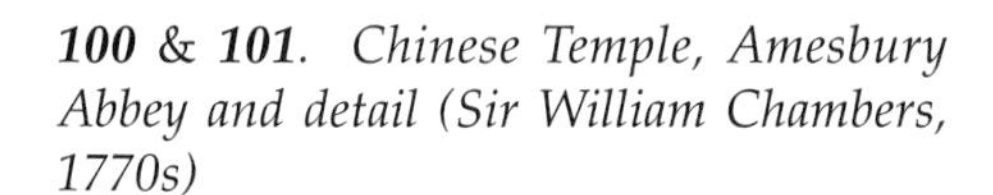

***100** & **101**. Chinese Temple, Amesbury Abbey and detail (Sir William Chambers, 1770s)*

The 1760s also saw work in Wiltshire by Robert Adam (1728-1792). He may have been jealous of William Chambers' social connections (see above) but he himself was hardly disadvantaged in his early years. His father William was himself an architect in Edinburgh and successful enough to be able to support Robert at Edinburgh University (where he mixed with the likes of Adam Smith and David Hume) and to fund an extended Grand Tour. He repaid this support by being a diligent student and traveller and, like Chambers or, as we shall see later, James Wyatt, was able to make a flying start to his architectural career. He was not only ambitious but had the confidence to challenge Palladian orthodoxy. At least, that is what he set out to do, and there is no doubt that much of his work, especially on internal design, is instantly recognisable as 'Robert Adam', but whether he did very much to halt the impetus of Palladianism is more arguable. His Wiltshire client was William Petty (1737-1805) who became 2nd Earl of Shelburne[2] in 1761. He was to become Prime Minister in 1784, with the unpopular task of steering through Parliament the terms for the loss of the American colonies, and, in 1784 (in recognition of his work), 1st Marquess of Lansdowne. The estate at Bowood had been acquired by his father, the 1st Earl, in 1754. It contained a large early-Georgian house ('the Big House') which had never been finished. The first Earl consulted Henry Keene (1726-76) who dramatised the building by adding two canted bays and a portico to the principal, south-facing side and

2. He is sometimes referred to as the 3rd Earl. This is because a great-uncle had been the original first Earl and his father's earldom had been of the second creation after a change of family name.

***102**. Mausoleum, Bowood (Robert Adam, 1761-65)*

added two service courts to the north-west. He also began a 'Great Room' on the north side. In 1761, Keene left England for Ireland and the 1st Earl died.

Upon his succession, the 2nd Earl's priority was a new house in London (Lansdowne House) for which he engaged Robert Adam; but he also used his services to complete the Big House and his mother commissioned Adam to build a mausoleum as a memorial to her late husband. A fourth family commission resulted in the closing of Keene's service courts by a long greenhouse (a correct, but misleading, description of the existing entrance front to the house). Indeed, there is much about Bowood that is difficult to follow; its own guide book states:

> No-one reading the history of Bowood could imagine that architects had an easy time with the 1st and 3rd Marquesses, who were the two people principally concerned with the creation of the House. They seemed to have constantly changed their minds as to what they wanted.

And in the midst of all this, Adam was engaged, from as early as 1761, on major work at Osterley Park and Syon House, Middlesex, as well as on many minor commissions. His first work at Bowood was the Mausoleum (1761-1765)[3]. Externally (fig.102) it is in the form of a Greek cross with a dome, that is to say, it is a square building with four short arms, one containing a tetrastyle portico with family arms in the pediment. For due solemnity, the

3. The Mausoleum is open to the public while the rhododendrons in the woodland gardens are in bloom, usually mid-May to the end of June.

***103**. Mausoleum, Bowood: interior (Robert Adam, 1761-65)*

simple Tuscan order is adopted. At the rear, a grass ramp leads down to the basement tomb-house which is only evident from that side. Internally (fig.103), the arms are tunnel-vaulted, separated from the central space by the entablature, which runs unbroken around the internal square, supported in each case by two Tuscan columns. Architectural enrichment is limited to niches, with a large *patera* above each one, and some scrolls in the corners of the ceilings. Now, Robert Adam's architecture, especially some of his sickly-sweet interiors are not to everybody's taste. But in this little building can be found the best of Adam and none of those elements that would later attract criticism. It combines the authority of Chambers with a delicacy that escaped the Burlingtonians. Not only is the design "of exceptional purity and nobility" (Pevsner), but, once again, it is an exhibition of Georgian craftsmanship at its best, without which the sublime effect could not have been achieved.

By 1765, Adam's alterations were complete but we need not dwell on these as the Big House was demolished in 1955. This was made easier by the existence of Adam's final contribution to Bowood, the closing of the service courts on their southern side by a long greenhouse, because what remains are two neat squares of buildings fronted by Adam's 'greenhouse', since converted into a series of rooms and galleries (fig.104). In the meantime, Capability Brown had been employed, by the 1st Earl initially,[4] to transform the grounds, including creating the large lake we see today to the east of the house. (A scheme for a

4. In 1757, the 1st Earl records "Mr Brown ... passed two days with me ... and 20 times assured me that he does not know a finer place in England than Bowood Park ... I am persuaded that the man means to present me at some future time with a well-digested plan for this place." (*Capability Brown and the 18th Century English Landscape* by Roger Turner).

104. *Bowood House before demolition of the 'Big House' (on the right) in 1955. (© Crown copyright, N.M.R.)*

bridge in the style of a Roman aqueduct, to be designed by Adam, did not come to fruition.) The major aesthetic effect of the removal of the Big House, as Roger Turner points out,[5] was to destroy the relationship of the house with the lake. However, to return to Adam's greenhouse, it was grandly dubbed 'the Diocletian Wing' because of the inspiration that Adam was known to have derived from the palace at Split. The long façade, fitted into the extremities of Keene's buildings, is colonnaded and arched, and articulated by a central, shallow portico (with two, widely-spaced pairs of columns) and two flat-headed pavilions with corner columns. There is much here that we have not seen before – the repetition of a semi-circular motif, the reeded design of the capitals, the closely packed balustrade and an overall lightness and delicacy that tell us that, here at least, we have moved on from Palladianism (fig.105).

105. *Bowood House: detail (Robert Adam, completed 1770)*

5. In *Capability Brown and the 18th Century English Landscape.*

This wing was completed in 1771, but a succession of architects were called in later: James Stuart (a chimney piece), Sir Robert Smirke (the Upper Terrace in front of the house), C.R.Cockerell (the chapel) and Charles Barry for, inter alia, the Clock Tower, which, unfortunately, only detracts from Adam's work, especially now it has attained greater prominence in the scheme of the house, following the demolition of the Big House. Adam's connections with this part of Wiltshire must end on a more painful note. In 1770, he was asked to design a new back range for Castle House, 7 Castle Street in nearby Calne. The property was acquired by the Borough Council in 1961; they were not allowed to demolish the building but they did nothing to preserve it and it was later demolished.[6] Adam's design looked ahead to the plainness of a house like Philipps House and was unusually unadorned both for Adam and for its age.

Another important architect at work in Wiltshire in the 1760s was Sir Robert Taylor (1714-1788). Unlike Robert Adam, he had entered architecture from the crafts (he had been apprenticed to the sculptor Sir Henry Cheere, brother of John Cheere) and had no wealth behind him at the start of his career. His father had paid for him to make a rather frugal visit to Italy but he had to return when he heard his father was dying (it is said that, to avoid detection as an Englishman, he travelled through France disguised as a Franciscan friar). He returned to find his father had died a bankrupt. Taylor had a few commissions in London but, realising he could not compete with the crop of fine sculptors active at the time, turned to architecture by the time he was 40. He worked immensely hard, often rising at four in the morning and also travelling at night so he could save time sleeping in the coach. He became so successful that another architect, Thomas Hardwick, said that Taylor and James Paine "nearly divided the practice of the profession between them ... till Mr.Robert Adam entered the list".[7] He served as a councillor in the City of London and his knighthood was bestowed when he became Sheriff in 1782. He would be best known by many later architects as the man who, with George Dance the Younger, drafted the London Building Act. His style was a no-frills, down-to-earth Palladianism; he particularly liked rusticated arches which he would use at Maidenhead Bridge and Salisbury Guildhall. His inspiration for this motif may have been Palladio's Palazzo Thiene in Vicenza, though this is a design in which the hand of the Mannerist Guilio Romano is thought to be present. He also liked the canted bay, a feature of, for example, Asgill House (1758-67) near Richmond, which can be seen standing prominently on the north bank of the Thames as you approach London on the A316. And we see it again, and some heavy rustication, in Chute House, Chute, in Wiltshire (but nearly in Hampshire), a house of the 1760s (figs.106 and 107) now divided into two

6. See Pevsner for what he calls "a deplorable story".
7. This state of affairs probably lasted from about 1753 to 1768, though Adam was certainly well launched on his own career by 1761.

106. Chute House, Chute (Sir Robert Taylor, 1760s)

residences after a long period in institutional use. It is difficult to imagine that either Taylor or Adam would have wished to be influenced by the work of the other.

James Paine (1717-89), already mentioned as Taylor's only rival for a time, was the son of a carpenter from Andover in Hampshire although most of his work was in the north of England. His style, too, was Palladian and it was only at the end of his career that he showed any desire to introduce some Adam-like touches into his work, and then only internally. Perhaps his grandest work is the one he undertook in Wiltshire at Wardour, near Tisbury, for Lord Arundell between 1770 and

107. Chute House: detail

108. *New Wardour Castle, near Tisbury (James Paine, 1770-76)*

1776. Old Wardour, the medieval castle enhanced by Smythson for Sir Matthew Arundell was mentioned in Chapter 4. By the 18th century, the old castle was considered only fit as a glorious ruin within the grounds of an appropriately fashionable mansion and so Lord Arundell commissioned Paine to design him a noble edifice on a site about a mile north-west of the old castle. He was the victim of *folie de grandeur;* he could not afford it and it nearly ruined him. But the house that Paine built (fig.108), now converted into flats after life as a girls' school for many years, is as cool an expression of English Palladianism as you could wish to see. Christopher Hussey has said of it "No building could be less open to the charge of pretentiousness – it is chastity itself". It consists of a weighty, nine-bay main block connected to smaller (but still substantial) three-bay pavilions by curving link blocks. There are many features to relish – the return to a distinct rustic and *piano nobile,* the great hexastyle portico, the Venetian windows set in a semi-circular headed frame and the use of Paine's favourite decorative ball motif along the top of the link blocks. It is also fascinating to see, in this palace-like building in the English countryside,

***109* & *110*.** *New Wardour Castle: detail of staircase*

tucked between the rich Corinthian capitals of the portico and the end twin pilasters, the small upper-tier windows that have come to us, via Palladio, from the vernacular farmhouses of Mediterranean lands. The building contains what Pevsner considered to be "the most glorious Georgian interior of Wiltshire", the central hall containing the staircase. Apart from the dramatic double, circular staircase, it is the richness of the circular gallery above and of the coffered dome and subsidiary apses that hold the eye (figs.109 and 110). The order is Corinthian and the monochrome decoration is suitably, and gloriously, elaborate. The western end of the complex holds the Catholic chapel, for which the main structure was designed by Paine, with later alterations by a young John Soane, but most of the interior design and fittings were much influenced, where not actually designed, by an Italian priest of Lord Arundell's acquaintance, Giacomo Quarenghi. Wardour had long been the principal centre in the

111. *The 'Dairy', New Wardour Castle (perhaps by John Soane)*

county for Catholic recusancy and the Arundells a prominent Catholic family. The chapel still has a thriving congregation today. Outside, not far from the chapel, can be found a small building (fig.111) used as a 'dairy' by the ladies of the house who could pretend they were engaged in honest rural labour. The architect's identity is not certain but the simplicity of the design and the curved portico shout 'Soane'.

So far in this chapter there has been no common theme to connect the various buildings described; each has been a 'one-off'. This variety is itself an indication that the old Palladian order was passing but only Adam's 'Diocletian Wing' contains any suggestion that a new one may be taking its place. And to conclude we will look at some work at Trafalgar Park in the 1760s that will confound the situation some more. But, first, what about Flitcroft's Temple of Apollo of 1765 (covered in Chapter 11)? Can it be called 'neo-classical'? It clearly stems from one of the new influences discussed in the previous chapter (Robert Wood's visit to Syria), but, on the 'archaeological' test, it is doubtful if it is right to call it neo-classical, such was Flitcroft's personal interpretation of what Wood had discovered. On the other hand, Sir William Chambers' version at Kew clearly is neo-classical because it was a conscious attempt – a unique one for him, Worsley suggests – to reproduce an ancient building (in a setting that was intended to be a sort of architectural World Fair).

The porch at Trafalgar Park (formerly Standlynch) is unequivocally neo-classical (figs.65, p.83, & 112). It was added for Henry Dawkins, the new owner of Standlynch, in 1766 and was designed by Nicholas Revett, the chronicler, with James Stuart, of Greek architecture. The porch is based on what Revett had seen at the Temple of Apollo at Delos. The Doric columns, in the Greek style, have no base – a feature that, when it first appeared, would be regarded as primitive and unrefined by those who had been brought up on the Roman version. Each column has a few inches of fluting at top and bottom but is otherwise plain. The clustering of the columns, as well as the spikiness which the decorative urns gives to its profile, have made the portico an inspired embellishment to John James's rather bland house. It is also an historically important structure as it was the first time, outside London, that the Greek orders had been used in England. Revett would not build the better-known Greek Portico at West Wycombe House for Sir Francis Dashwood until 1771. This is readily explained by the fact that Dawkins was not only, like Dashwood, a member of the Dilettanti Society (whose members took a close interest in any archaeological evidence of antiquity, whether Greek or Roman) but James Dawkins, Henry's late brother, had accompanied Robert Wood to Syria and would have known Revett. Another companion had been John Bouverie, a member of the family that had bought Longford Castle, just two miles or so from Standlynch,

112. *Trafalgar Park, Standlynch: porch (Nicholas Revett, 1766)*

***113**. Trafalgar Park, Standlynch: south wing (John Wood the Younger, c.1766)*

in 1717. Bouverie had died in the course of the journey and was buried at Smyrna in 1750.

Now, the portico at Standlynch may have been a pioneering work, untypical of its period, but it only formed a small part of the changes being made at that time. Dawkins was also adding north and south wings (fig.113) to the house and for these he commissioned John Wood the Younger. Each could be a separate house in its own right but linked to the main house by a corridor. The style is demure, in tune with the main block; although the added buildings are quite large, they do not either overpower or detract from the original building. Each block derives its own interest from a canted bay on its outer side and a three-bay projection in the middle of its inner side. Dawkins, with the wealth he had acquired in the West Indies and had inherited both from his brother James and an uncle of the same name, had managed to turn Standlynch into an impressive and unusual range of buildings in the best traditions of the Palladian villa.

14 Some Public Commissions

We have still not quite finished with the 1760s because two contrasting public ventures were begun late in that decade. One was by a Bath architect in Salisbury and the other was by a non-Bath architect in Bath. Ideas had been formulated in Salisbury for a new public infirmary and a committee was formed in 1766 under the chairmanship of William Bouverie, 1st Earl of Radnor, who would become the first President of the 'Governors of the General Infirmary at Salisbury, for the Relief of the Sick and Lame Poor, from whatever county recommended'. Another prominent subscriber, Henry Herbert, 10th Earl of Pembroke, would become its first 'Visitor'. Other subscribers' names that have already appeared on these pages (or will soon do so) as patrons of architecture are Henry Wyndham, James Harris, Lord Bruce, the Duke and Duchess of Queensbury, Henry Dawkins, Paul Methuen, Henry Hoare and Thomas Benett (of Pythouse – see Chapter 16). It may be significant that Lord Arundell, with his grandiose plans for a new house and grounds at Wardour (see Chapter 13), committed himself to a legacy in his will but not to any payments during his lifetime. The chosen architect was John Wood the Younger, perhaps through the Dawkins connection, and he was soon being thanked by the Governors for "his ingenious plan for a building". (He too became a subscriber). The foundation stone was laid in 1767. This was the year work also began on the Royal Crescent and Wood was still involved with Brock Street and, probably, the wing extensions at Standlynch. The Upper Assembly Rooms would be started only two years later, the Infirmary not being completed until 1771.

The term 'infirmary' was used at that time for what were, in effect, hospitals to distinguish them from the medieval 'hospitals' which were usually what we now call almshouses. The modern hospital in Britain derives from the humanitarian ideals of the 18th-century Enlightenment. (We have seen how, in Bath, those ideals may not have been unalloyed by other motives but the Mineral Water Hospital *was* catering for rather special needs in a spa town.) The form that one of these new infirmaries should take posed an interesting challenge to their architects. Early examples of hospital buildings were the Foundling (1742) by Theodore Jacobsen, the London (1748) by Boulton Mainwaring and the Middlesex (1752) by James Paine. As Sir John Summerson pointed out in *The Architecture of the Eighteenth Century*, it cannot be said that any distinct architectural type for hospitals emerged. Plain brick façades with a central pediment were the usual thing, compositional ideas being very much those applicable to large country houses. Wood's Salisbury Infirmary, however, was an exception, comprising a square mass with a central light-well, a crenellated parapet and windows all of equal size (fig.114). The design is virtually identical to one for the façade of a house amongst a set of miscellaneous

114. *Salisbury Infirmary: north façade elevation (John Wood the Younger, 1767). (Wiltshire and Swindon Record Office)*

drawings in Bath Public Library by the Elder and Younger Wood. Even after extensions and improvements had been effected in the 19th century (including some with the advice of Florence Nightingale who had been brought in by her friend Sidney Herbert), the Infirmary remained a pleasant and spacious site on the edge of town. The writer W.H.Hudson described it, in *A Shepherd's Life* (published in 1910), as "That great comely building of warm, red brick in Fisherton Street, set well back so that you can see it as a whole, behind its

115. *Salisbury Infirmary after restoration*

cedar and beech trees ..." Well, the trees did not last much longer, the site filled up with more buildings and the original building suffered all kinds of indignities in the face of modern requirements until the whole enterprise eventually began again on another site. The Infirmary and the best of its ancillary buildings have been sympathetically adapted to (mainly) residential use and it is still possible to make out John Wood's original building (fig.115). What is remarkable is that, throughout more than two centuries of alterations to the building, the original stone inscription still remains; it reads: GENERAL INFIRMARY SUPPORTED BY VOLUNTARY CONTRIBUTION 1767.

While Robert Adam was still engaged in his comings and goings at Bowood, he was having a frustrating time in trying to apply his talents in nearby Bath. His patron there was William Pulteney and it may have been he who invited Adam to submit his unsuccessful scheme for the Upper Assembly Rooms. It was certainly Pulteney who invited him to design a prison on some of his land on the east side of the river Avon but again the scheme of a local man was preferred. But meanwhile, Pulteney had acquired the power, through an Act of Parliament, to build a new bridge over the Avon to enable his land on the east side to be developed as a new Bath suburb. For this, he was able to commission Robert Adam. It was begun in 1769 and was opened in 1774 (fig.116). For all his anxiety to avoid the Palladian *style* it seems probable that Adam was strongly influenced by a design of Palladio, namely, that already mentioned in Chapter 9, his unsuccessful design for the Rialto in Venice. Here we see the same pedimented central feature and pavilions set on the banks (subject to what is said below about the south-western one), the same three semi-circular

***116**. Pulteney Bridge, Bath (Robert Adam, 1769-74)*

arches and even (uniquely in England) the same rows of shops – not four, as in Palladio's design, but two, one on each side of a carriageway. However, the way it is all put together is distinctly Adam rather than Palladio with little domes on the four end pavilions, the frequent repetition of the semi-circular motif and an astylar smoothness that is elegant without being bland. The bridge had been in a sorry state when Ison first wrote about it soon after the war, with a mass of minor alterations and ugly accretions, but sterling efforts have since been made to restore it to something like its original state. (The major missing elements are the narrow loggias – four in all – that faced outwards from the pavilions at each end of the structure. Also one bay of the structure at its south-western end was removed in 1908, making the sides of unequal length and the south side assymetrical; the terminal pavilion was rebuilt but now stands less distinctly on the river bank than do the other three.) This was to be Adam's first and last commission in Bath. Pulteney invited him to draw up plans for the development of his estate but, once again, he would be thwarted; his patron died, the estate passed to his daughter, Henrietta Laura, and she decided to adopt rival plans submitted by Thomas Baldwin. The only other public memento of Adam in Bath is a wine cooler which he designed, to be found in the Mayor's Parlour in the Guildhall.

In Bath, the 1770s continued to be dominated by John Wood but with Thomas Baldwin unexpectedly coming to prominence, as the architect to the Corporation's estates, in 1775. This had resulted from the untimely death of the previous incumbent of that office, Thomas Warr Atwood (c.1733-1775). He was a wealthy builder and plumber and one of the many accusations levelled at him during the Guildhall fiasco (soon to come) was that he had exerted undue influence to obtain his official position. What *will* seem extraordinary to anyone familiar with present day conditions of service of local government officers is that he then proceeded to secure Corporation leases for his own building enterprises at The Paragon, London Road and Oxford Row, Lansdown Road (opposite Belmont). On the other hand, the Corporation approved the designs and no doubt felt that to have their own appointee to execute the work was the best guarantee of a successful outcome. It was Atwood who, in preference to Robert Adam, secured the commission for the prison in Grove Street;[1] work began in 1772. If the proportions at first appear a little odd (fig.117), it is because the surface of Grove Street was meant to have been built to a higher level than it was and this would have had the effect of making the whole of the present ground floor lower than the street. The design is Palladian but the way the floors relate to each other is unusual. The ground floor (i.e. the one above the 'basement') is vigorously rusticated to make it appear that it consists of large, distinct, blocks of stone in a suitably menacing manner; above it are three pedestals of diminishing area and then a projecting band on which

1. The former prison had been in an old church tower pulled down to build Pulteney Bridge.

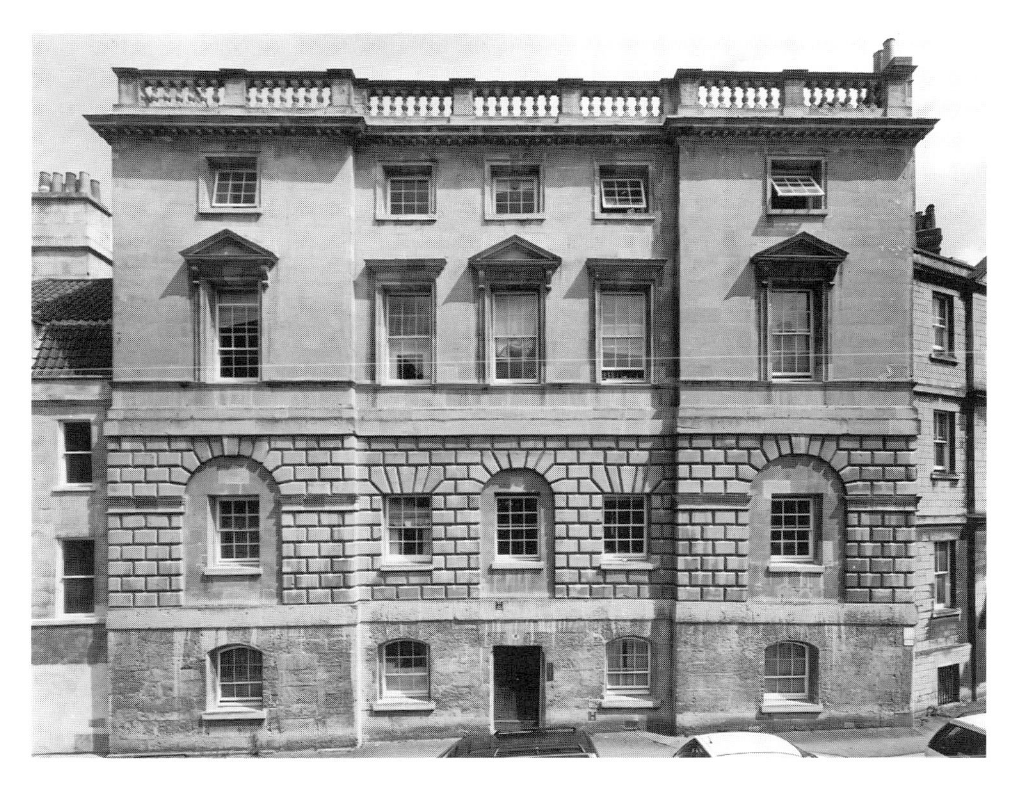

117. Former prison, Grove Street, Bath (Thomas Atwood, begun 1772) (© Crown copyright, N.M.R.)

rest the windows of the first floor. It is as if the two upper floors (including the elegant balustrade above the projecting cornice) have been set down on top of the ground floor and could just as easily be lifted off again by some giant hand. This might have been welcomed by its original inmates but the building is now converted into flats.

Atwood's most prestigious project would have been the Guildhall. His design for it was approved in 1775. A rival proposal was put forward by John Palmer and Thomas Jelly which they claimed would be less burdensome on the public purse to the tune of £6,000. But when work began in 1776, it was to yet another design – that of Thomas Baldwin. Despite massive public vilification of Atwood and although an arbitration (on the matter of cost) came down in favour of Palmer and Jelly, the Corporation stuck by its man. But then Atwood suddenly met his death by falling through the floor of an old house due to be demolished for the Guildhall scheme. Thomas Baldwin (1750-1820) had been his assistant on a number of projects, and, at the age of 25, was appointed to take his place as city architect and was instructed to prepare new plans for the Guildhall. He would continue to hold official Corporation appointments until his own downfall in 1793. His design for the building is as we see it today (fig.118) except for the wings and the dome which were added in 1891 to the design of J.M.Brydon. This was the first of a series of prominent buildings by Baldwin that announced the coming of a new generation and represented a

***118**. The Guildhall, Bath (Thomas Baldwin, begun 1776)*

new approach. But it hardly amounted to a revolution. The difference in mood between, say, Widcombe Manor, that charming hang-over from the 17th century, but actually started in about 1727, and the north side of Queen Square – started in 1728 – is far greater than that between Queen Square and the Guildhall (started in 1776). Nearly 50 years after Queen Square we still see a building designed with a rusticated ground floor, a central portico with engaged giant columns and pedimented windows. The influence of Adam is clear enough – the blind semi-circular arches in which the upper-floor tabernacle windows are set, the 'pretty' garland motifs in the pediment and in the panels on each side of the portico frieze, the fluting in the frieze itself – but it is hardly a rejection of Bath's Palladian tradition. And this is about as far as things go under Baldwin: a recognition that a new, more delicate style is in fashion but without any radical departure from an accepted norm. It is a style that seems to suit Bath very well and provides some much-needed contrast to what had gone before. The Guildhall is one of the city's best buildings and contains what is one of its most important Georgian interior spaces, the magnificent Banqueting Hall. It is also a building with a well-designed rear elevation with which the architect has taken as much trouble as he has with the front façade (fig.119).

It is to the more familiar Bath Palladianism and to John Wood the Younger that we return for the moment. It was in the 1770s that the streets around the Upper Assembly Rooms were laid out by Wood beginning with Arthur Street, Bennett Street and Russell Street all, by now 'typical', Bath terraced streets, severely elegant with just a few minor design variations from each other and from what had gone before. The most pleasing is Russell Street with three-bay houses (with some variations in design), stepped up the sloping site, the view upwards being closed by a three-bay bow in Rivers Street. This too was a John Wood development extending westwards to Catherine Place, which was also his. By now we have swung right back to the longitude of the west end of Brock Street so there is hardly a building in the great swathe of streets from the Royal Crescent to the east end of Bennett Street in which Wood did not have a hand.

***119**. The Guildhall, Bath: rear elevation, detail*

In 1775 he was given a more interesting challenge – a commission from the Corporation for the building of the Hot Bath.[2] For such an important spa town, little had been done over the last 50 years to modernise its bathing arrangements. However, the building of the Hot Bath was a start and many more improvements, mainly by Baldwin, followed. The building, currently (2000) undergoing restoration as part of the Bath Spa Millennium Project, is an unpretentious, single-storey, square block of which the most notable feature is its sober Roman Doric portico. But where Wood excelled was in the internal design with a series of dressing rooms and private facilities arranged symmetrically (along both main axes) around the Hot Bath itself. This arrangement was destroyed by later generations but it had represented a good step forward in the design of the city's baths and it will be a treat to see it restored.

2. This was Wood's only commission for the Corporation. The commission for the Upper Assembly Rooms was from a group of private individuals who had formed theselves into a tontine.

***120**. Former Hardenhuish House, Chippenham (John Wood the Younger, 1770s)*

Wood had also been busy in Wiltshire, designing a country mansion for Joseph Colborne at Hardenhuish, now swallowed up by Chippenham but then a separate settlement. The building (fig.120) is now the sixth form centre of Hardenhuish School. It is an unremarkable Palladian design with a large canted bay on its eastern side. The curved porch is a later addition (for Thomas Clutterbuck) and is almost certainly by Sir John Soane, whose hand has also been detected in some of the internal treatment. About half a mile to the west of the house is St.Nicholas's Church, Hardenhuish, also by Wood (with, again, Joseph Colborne as client), built in 1779 (fig.121). Pevsner tells us that Wood's original design had included polygonal apses both at the east and west ends, making the plan more central than the one to which it was built. It is a charming small building in the classical style – everyone's idea of a Georgian church – but spoilt by the abrupt straightness of the west front. Nor has its appearance been improved by the 'filling in' in 1856 of the area east of the tower to provide more space inside. A model in the church shows the original, more sinuous shape of the building (fig.122). The east end of the churchyard contains a striking monument of 1823 to the politician and economist, David Ricardo – all Greek with mourning maidens.

Bath once had a number of Georgian-style churches, including some by both John Woods, but the only ones to have survived are Timothy Lightoler's Octagon Chapel, Milsom Street (so difficult, in its setting and museum use, to appreciate either inside or out) and John Palmer's St.Swithin's, Walcot. St.Swithin's was begun in 1777 but the tower and spire were not added

121. St.Nicholas's Church, Hardenhuish, Chippenham (John Wood the Younger, 1779)

until 1790. Most of the interest in the church derives from those elements, a series of geometric shapes adorned with classical features. The body of the church has been simply, but effectively, divided by giant Corinthian pilasters

122. St.Nicholas's Church, Hardenhuish, Chippenham: model showing its original shape

into six bays, each containing a large round-headed window and a smaller window, with a curved top, below a projecting band about one third of the way up the wall.

There is a feeling about both St.Nicholas's and St.Swithin's that they fall between two stools: they lack, on the one hand, the excitement of a church by Wren or Hawksmoor or Gibbs yet also lack the simplicity of the Non-Conformist chapel in which the classical idiom is often used with great success (Palmer's own Presbyterian chapel of 1795 in Trim Street is a case in point). Palladianism does not seem well suited to the churches of the age even though it may have been just the thing for country villas or for the urban terraces of Bath. But this may be to ignore the spirit of that age. In *English Parish Churches,*[3] Graham Hutton places St.Nicholas's in a group of temple-like churches of the Georgian period which he considers "infinitely charming". "The language they speak", he suggests, "is at one in clarity and commonsense with Locke's philosophy and advocacy of tolerance. It was as perfectly keyed to its age as was the Early English style to the thirteenth century."

3. In Thames and Hudson's *The World of Art Library* series.

15 Palladianism on the Wane – 1780 to 1800

By 1780, Palladianism, as it would have been understood by those that revived it in Britain earlier in the century, had largely disappeared. In Bath, Baldwin had adopted the trappings of the Adam style and the only buildings of any significance in Wiltshire in the next 20 years would be Salisbury Guildhall, Sir Robert Taylor's swan-song, an extension to St.Edmund's College, Salisbury and two houses by James Wyatt who had his own style, or rather styles, that were certainly not pure Palladian. Yet, all the same, as we shall see, there was still a great deal of Palladian endeavour to come in Bath and, for the moment, it is only Baldwin, and, perhaps, Eveleigh, in his own quirky way, who will try to show that there is life after Palladianism. Baldwin's first private building venture was Northumberland Buildings begun in about 1780. This terrace (fig.123) completes the south side of Wood Street where it leads into Queen Square so it is easy to compare it on site with the earlier work of John Wood the Elder. First, the windows account for much more space within the front façade than in those of Queen Square but the fenestration is, in fact, little different from the style adopted by, say Atwood or the younger Wood. Next, the attic, instead of being tucked discreetly into the roof space, stands out flush with the principal floors below (an arrangement much valued, no doubt, by the servants who lived in those uppermost rooms). The overweighty appearance that this gives would not

123. Northumberland Buildings, Wood Street, Bath (Thomas Baldwin, begun c.1780)

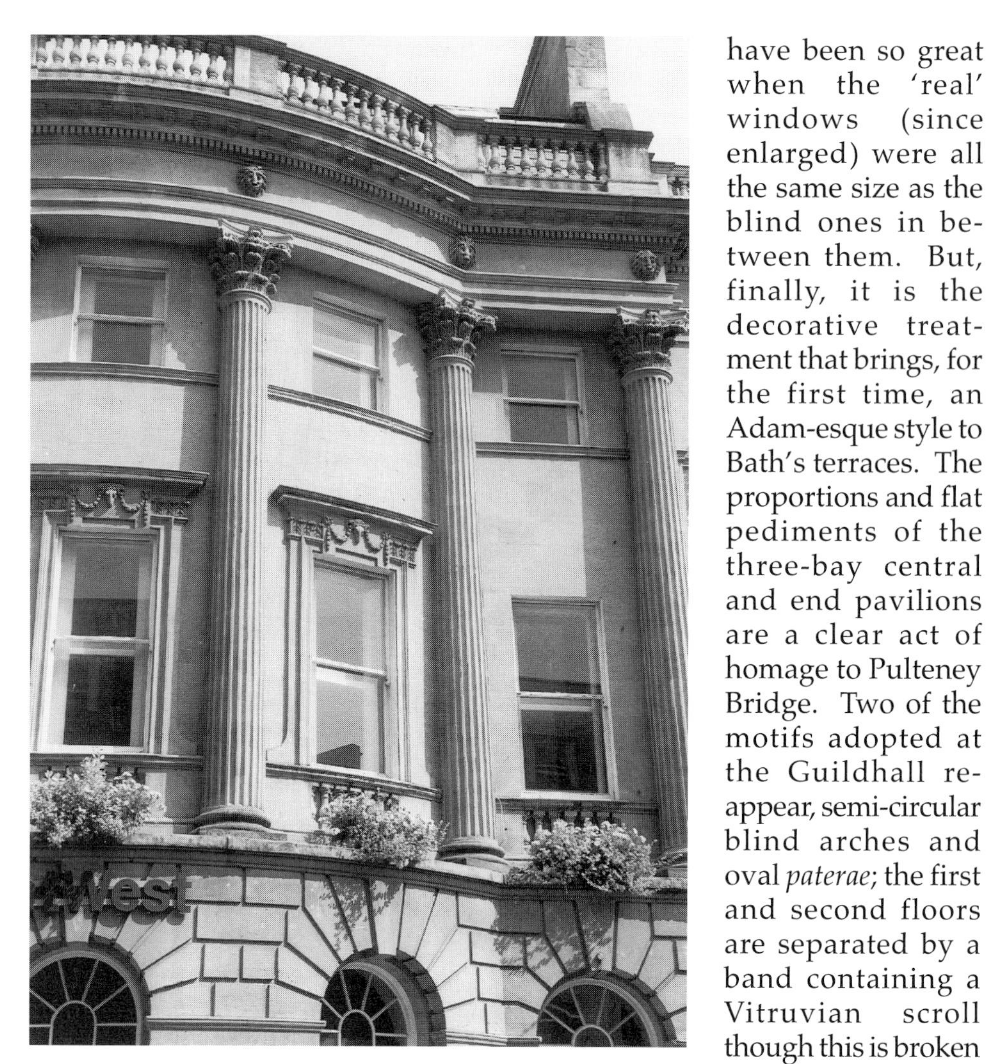

124. *Somersetshire Buildings, Milsom Street, Bath (Thomas Baldwin, 1781-83): detail of central bowed pavilion*

have been so great when the 'real' windows (since enlarged) were all the same size as the blind ones in between them. But, finally, it is the decorative treatment that brings, for the first time, an Adam-esque style to Bath's terraces. The proportions and flat pediments of the three-bay central and end pavilions are a clear act of homage to Pulteney Bridge. Two of the motifs adopted at the Guildhall reappear, semi-circular blind arches and oval *paterae*; the first and second floors are separated by a band containing a Vitruvian scroll though this is broken by a festooned arch in each of the end pavilions and, in the central three bays, by the entablature of four, barely noticeable, pilasters, the first pilasters to appear on a terrace in Bath since John Wood the Elder's north side of Queen Square. From these small beginnings would grow the giant pilasters of Bathwick!

Another early work of Baldwin was Somersetshire Buildings, Milsom Street (1781-83). This range of buildings is sometimes criticised for being too showy in a street of an otherwise plain Palladian style but, given the prestigious nature of what has become Bath's principal shopping and commercial street, the curvaceous grandeur of Baldwin's contribution does not go amiss. It is a powerful composition with a rusticated ground floor (not all of which has avoided the insertion of shop fronts) and the upper two floors bristling with Corinthian giant engaged columns, five in a central pavilion (containing a three-bay bow) and four in each end pavilion supporting a pediment. The three pavilions are linked by three-bay astylar blocks. Windows are either totally plain or are set in tabernacle frames (fig.124). These frames alone contain a touch of the Adam-esque for otherwise the composition is more of an elegant variation on the theme of the north side of Queen Square. For the next few years, Baldwin's professional life would be dominated by his official duties. He had been appointed Deputy Chamberlain in 1778 and, in 1779, was made Inspector of Baths (continuing to be re-appointed annually as City Architect). In about 1786, he undertook a re-construction of the Cross Bath – all lightness and delicacy in contrast to John Wood the Younger's nearby Hot Bath – and, north of the Pump Room (the building that later made way for the Great Pump Room), he built the colonnade that encloses Abbey Yard where it joins Stall Street.

By the end of the 1770s, housing development in Lansdown Road had been extended further up the hill with the building of the Belvedere terrace, London Road's development had reached Walcot Terrace (facing the site of the future Cleveland Bridge) and, in the south-western sector of the city, the great length of New King Street had been built. Bath was now ready to push on up Lansdown Hill and across the river to Bathwick. Baldwin would direct his energies to Bathwick while John Palmer and John Eveleigh would be the architects primarily involved with the hillside terraces. The first development on the hillside was Burlington Street, climbing straight up the hill from Julian Road and, running along the contour at the top to form a 'T', Portland Place, both begun in about 1786. The designer may have been John Eveleigh. His dates are unknown but he was a contemporary of both Baldwin and Palmer. Colvin thinks he is probably the "John Eveley" apprenticed to James Paine in 1756. He worked in Bath from the late 1780s until about 1793. Eveleigh is also the likely architect of the first major crescent in Bath following the example of the Royal Crescent, namely Camden Crescent which leads roughly northwards off Lansdown Road. This was begun in 1788 but gives not the slightest nod of recognition to the new influences that have made Baldwin's work so distinctive. The design is purely Palladian with a central, temple-like block of four bays (meaning that it contains an 'incorrect' central column, probably to cater for the dividing line between housing units going down the centre of the block) and more Corinthian, engaged columns in an end pavilion. There is only one because, after a landslip, the northern end was never completed. The remainder of the terrace is enriched, above a rusticated ground floor, by Corinthian pilasters.

A third major architect in Bath at this period, alongside Baldwin and Eveleigh, was John Palmer (c.1738-1817). His father Thomas had been a glazier who worked with Thomas Jelly. In 1765, Jelly took John Palmer into partnership with him and we have seen their work at St.James's Parade. In 1792 he would succeed Baldwin as City Architect. His principal works after St.James's Parade were St.James's church (demolished) and St.Swithin's church. His first major housing commission, Lansdown Crescent, was not

125. 'Rus in urbe': Lansdown Crescent and Lansdown Place West (John Palmer, begun 1789)

begun until 1789. Bath had leapt across the river the year before, with the start of the development of the Pulteney Estate, and would now make another great leap, this time to a much higher part of the hill. The Ordnance Survey map shows countour lines packed closely together below Lansdown Crescent and also very few buildings in that particular part of Bath. These two facts are, of course, not unrelated. The only significant later infill here would be St.James's Square. In its towering location, Lansdown Crescent is, in some ways, even more dramatic than the Royal Crescent. Being even further removed from the bustle of the town – and the gap would have been larger when it was built than it is today – it has a strange mixture of rurality (heightened by the sight of sheep grazing in the huge meadow below) and sophisticated urban elegance (fig.125). Thus it conveys an air of unreality, like an elaborate film set waiting for something to happen. The buildings snake along the contour and comprise three elements: the Crescent proper, in the shape of roughly a third of a circle (like the sections of the Circus without the pulling in of the ends as at the Royal Crescent) and, on each side, across a narrow lane giving access to mews to the rear, a curving wing (Lansdown Place East and Lansdown Place West)[1] but now curving outwards instead of inwards. The main interest lies in the Crescent with a pedimented centre and end pavilions containing three-bay bows. The pediment is supported by two pairs of plain Ionic pilasters allowing room

1. The bridge-like structure across the westernmost lane (seen in fig.125) was built by H.E.Goodridge for William Beckford between the two houses he acquired here when he quit Fonthill Abbey; it forms part of the right-hand house and does not function as a link.

***126**. St.James's Square, Bath: north side (John Palmer, 1790-93 – a pity about the plainness*

in the centre of the first floor for an additional, taller, round-headed window to push itself in between two standard windows in a semi-Venetian arrangement. Horizontal emphases are provided by a plain plat band above the rusticated ground floor, a scrolled band above the first floor and, at the top of the façade, a balustrade with urns on the pavilions. Again, there is no outward trace of any desire to depart from Bath Palladianism.

Nor would there be in Palmer's next commission, St.James's Square, built between 1790 and 1793. (Neither Palmer nor Eveleigh, in the developments we are looking at here, were the developers in the manner of either of the Woods, for example, but were acting as architects for others.) At St.James's Square, many of the Palladian motifs used at Lansdown Crescent can be seen again, but the general form of the development is quite different, being an urban square, in the tradition of Queen Square, with a terrace of houses on each side and an open space, or garden, behind railings, in the centre. The 'Square' is actually a rectangle, with the longer sides running north/south. Being tucked away behind the Royal Crescent, it carries far less intrusive traffic than Queen Square but its character is still eroded by the inevitable rows of parked cars on both sides of its carriageways. An interesting touch is that its four approach roads join the corners of the square at an oblique angle. The architectural arrangement (so far as the trees in the garden allow you to see it) resembles Queen Square in that the the north and south sides are grander compositions than the other two; indeed Palmer has borrowed from Lansdown Crescent the pedimented centre and end pavilions containing a bow (fig.126). But that is about as far as any comparison goes.

***127**. St.James's Square, Bath, west side: detail of the southern pavilion*

The motifs have been cleverly re-articulated for this less equivocally urban site though it has to be said that the use of Composite order capitals without any enrichment elsewhere suggests that there may have been some compromises made between developer and architect. The difficulty about the east and west sides are that they seem overlong; the centre and end houses are designed as somewhat grander pavilions with some rustication and elaborate framing of the first floor windows (fig.127); this makes them attractive features in themselves but they are too small and too far apart from each other to make any cohesive sense. But, for all its missed opportunities, St.James's Square gives a fine taste of late 18th-century Bath and should not be missed on any 'architectural' visit to the town.

At about the time Palmer was engaged at Lansdown Crescent, another terrace was being built to the west and along the same contour line. This was Somerset Place, by John Eveleigh, consisting of a shallow crescent with a central, six-bay pavilion surmounted by an open-topped elliptical pediment (fig.128). With an urn in the open centre and a string of Adamesque decorative features, the pediment makes the central block look like a huge piece of Georgian furniture but the whole effect is another charming addition to Bath's rich architectural heritage. Its other unusual feature is the use of heads (or masks) in the keystones of the doorways, a device much loved in Italy but less common in England, except in Baroque buildings. (Another example can be found at the Fonthill Archway.) Expansion was also taking place in the south of the city (though still north of the river) with Green Park and Seymour Street and, further west, beyond New King Street, with Norfolk Crescent. This has an impressive but lonely air as, with its back to the city centre, it seems to be facing a future in the west that never took place. All these developments are attributed to John Palmer. London Road was also extended with what proved to be the over-ambitious Grosvenor Park scheme begun in 1791 of which only Grosvenor Place was completed. This comprises a terrace incorporating as a central feature a highly ornamented and unusual hotel building (fig.129). The development has attracted varied comments ranging from "Eveleigh's masterpiece" (Ison) to "a formless mass of styles and solecisms" (Bryan Little[2]). Colvin hedges his bets when he says that Eveleigh's use of "Adamsian motifs in an almost baroque manner ... is engagingly vigorous or vulgarly inelegant according to taste".

***128**. Somerset Place, Bath: central pavilion (John Eveleigh, begun c.1790)*

***129**. Former Grosvenor Hotel, Grosvenor Place, London Road, Bath (John Eveleigh, begun 1791)*

2. In *The Building of Bath, 47 to 1947.*

So now we cross the river to one of Bath's most remarkable developments, that of the Pulteney Estate in the area known as Bathwick. What Baldwin planned for the estate is very different from what was achieved before bankruptcy overtook him in 1793. This followed from the collapse of the Bath City Bank (and it was the same disaster that forced John Eveleigh to cease working in Bath and to move to Plymouth, where he was last heard of). Had he been working merely in the capacity of an architect (like John Palmer at St.James's Square) he would no doubt have survived, but he had taken leases of land from Henrietta Pulteney and was acting as its developer. Baldwin's estate plan was on similar lines to those produced for William Pulteney by Robert Adam and would have allowed Bath's expansion to spread out from the east end of Pulteney Bridge like a fan. The first piece of building, Argyle Buildings (now Argyle Place) in 1788 was unworthy of its location or of what was to come. But Baldwin himself designed Laura Place and Henrietta Street and continued the style he had developed there down Great Pulteney Street. And a fine self-confident style it was – basically Palladian but with traces of the motifs he had used successfully at the Guildhall and Somersetshire Buildings. Before the crash, he managed to complete Great Pulteney Street, one terrace flanking Sydney Gardens (Sydney Place), two short terraces in Bathwick Street and some short returns in streets off Great Pulteney Street that stand isolated and unfinished.

In Laura Place we see the huge (but thin) Corinthian fluted pilasters and the ground-floor rustication that first appeared in Bath's terraces at Queen Square (north side) but here it is all done with a much greater delicacy: more like thin decorative icing on a cake than an integral part of the building. And then the theme is carried on down Great Pulteney Street – 'great' indeed with a length of 1100 feet and a width of 100 feet[3] – with terraces so long it is hard to make sense of them. Indeed the north-eastern one has got a pediment missing at one point; this (and the removal of some parapets and balustrades) may have occurred during a period after the war when a relaxed attitude was being taken towards alterations that might help to encourage the use of unoccupied living accommodation. The spaciousness and the classical rhythms give it the feel of a Roman triumphal way or, perhaps, a Royal Mall in a capital city. For a provincial spa town, Bath is indeed a remarkable place! For the adjoining Sydney Place and Bathwick Street, Baldwin changes down a gear or two and we return to the normal scale and rhythms of Bath. In Sydney Place, he uses a form of vermiculated rustication for the doorway surround that Sir Robert Taylor would have been proud of (fig.130). In Bathwick Street, the tone has become very modest after the grandeur of Great Pulteney Street but the treatment of the façade is still of interest, in the way the triple windows have been articulated and, on the first floor, enriched in a style that is unique in Bath (fig.131).

3. A metric conversion would not seem appropriate here!

130 & ***131***. *(left) No.10 Sydney Place, Bath (Thomas Baldwin, 1792): door surround. (right) No.21 Bathwick Street, Bath (Thomas Baldwin, 1792)*

Baldwin would lose his official appointments, first, through accusations of slow progress with the improvements to the baths and, finally, through a failure to submit official accounts, but not before he had undertaken work in the very heart of the city that remains the backdrop to much of its daily activity and an essential part of its character. The first was the 'New Private Baths' (1788), now called the King's and Queen's Baths, followed, in 1790, by the Great Pump Room and Bath Street.[4] He also did work in Stall Street, Cheap Street and Union Street which has either been altered or replaced. The western side of the Great Pump Room (in Stall Street) flanked by pedimented colonnades (fig.132) is a sequence of great richness and quality that cannot help but lift the spirits of the visitor to Bath. The influence of Adam abounds, in the *paterae*, the sphinxes, the festoons and so on, but there is still a Palladian solidity to the rusticated lower half of the Great

4. See Ison for a full account of these buildings and of Baldwin's financial and other difficulties at this time.

132. *Stall Street, Bath, with (foreground) King's and Queen's Baths (1788) and Great Pump Room and colonnades (1790) (Thomas Baldwin)*

Pump Room wall and the heavy engaged columns above. And turning round, all is different again, with the cool elegance of Bath Street, which the Corporation laid out itself (under local Act powers) to the design of Baldwin. Here, at last, was an arrangement worthy of a great spa town – a colonnaded street providing a covered link between the Hot and Cross Baths at one end and Abbey Yard and the Great Pump Room at the other (fig.133). Bath was already, by then, suffering from competition from other spa towns and from the new fashion of sea-bathing (pioneered by George III at Weymouth – ironically, with the assistance and advice of Ralph Allen) but we must be glad that this ensemble of buildings was created while the will and the funds still existed and while the services of Baldwin were still available.

However, his position as City Architect was finally removed in 1792 and, in 1793, John Palmer was appointed in his place. It fell to him to complete the Great Pump Room and it is probable that the designs of the main façade and of the Pump Room itself are his rather than Baldwin's. The columns of the engaged portico are consistent with the western façade and the oval windows are similar to those used by Baldwin in the rear elevation of the Guildhall to light the Banqueting Room but, overall, it seems to fall short of what could be expected from Baldwin himself had he been allowed to finish it. This, of course, is the place where the waters may be taken (not to mention tea, in gracious surroundings) and the Greek inscription, in praise of water, is there to remind us in the portico frieze.[5]

5. Rendered as ΑΡΙΣΤΟΝ ΜΕΝ Υ[c]ΔΩΡ ('Ariston men Hudor' – 'Water is Best').

***133**. Bath Street, Bath (1790) with Cross Bath (1784; rebuilt c.1790) (Thomas Baldwin)*

134. Guildhall, Salisbury: original design for the north elevation (Sir Robert Taylor, 1788). (Wiltshire and Swindon Record Office)

Just four years after work began on Bath Guildhall, Salisbury also was suddenly faced with the need to provide a new home for its City Council. In 1780, during the night after the annual mayoral dinner at the Council House in the Market Place, the old building went up in flames. Lord Radnor, the City's Recorder, generously agreed to fund the reconstruction of the building but he stipulated that it should be erected on a new site right in the middle of the Market Place. Wisely, the Council demurred and set about seeking another solution; it was eventually agreed with the Bishop that his, virtually redundant, Guildhall (a hangover from the days when the Bishop was 'Lord of the City' which only came to an end in 1612) should be demolished and the new Council House built on its site. Work began, in the south-eastern corner of the Market Place, in 1788. The architect was Sir Robert Taylor who produced the design but died a few days before the foundation stone was laid. The building was completed in 1795 and by then alterations had already been made to Taylor's design by his pupil William Pilkington who had become responsible for the execution. Taylor would have had Venetian windows in the front elevation (figs.134 & 135) but these were changed to large single windows. More significantly, in 1829-30, the row of columns in front of a recessed centre were re-formed into a flat-topped portico standing in front of the building (fig.136). The architect was Thomas Hopper. In 1889, a projecting portico on the west side was removed.

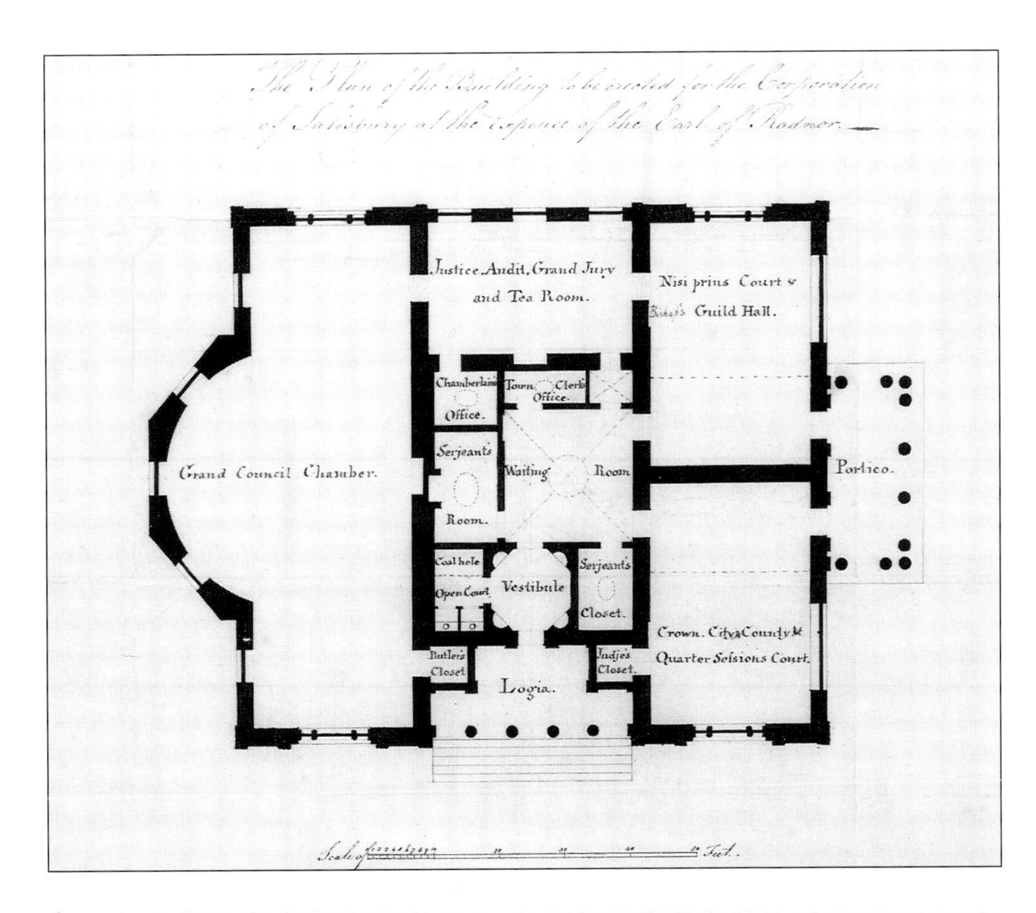

135. *Guildhall Salisbury: original ground plan. (Wiltshire and Swindon Record Office)*

136. *Guildhall, Salisbury from the north-west (Sir Robert Taylor, 1788, with alterations by William Pilkington (1788-95) and by Thomas Hopper (1829-30))*

137. Guildhall, Salisbury from the south-east: a photograph of 1942 when Fish Row and Butcher Row were still thoroughfares. (© Crown copyright, N.M.R.)

Despite these changes, the building remains full of interest and unique in its conception. James Stevens Curl, writing about Taylor, says:

> at his Guildhall in Salisbury of 1788 he gave England one of its first truly grand Local Government buildings. This extra-ordinary free-standing single-storey[6] building employs Taylor's favourite vermiculated rusticated quoins and voussoirs, has Serlians set in the powerful blocky elements of the design, and in the Council Chamber [now the Banqueting Room] a bow contained within a canted bay [see figs.137 & 138]. The entrance was approached through a screen of unfluted Roman Doric columns set between the projecting wings. Central rooms were top-lit, like parts of the Bank of England. In this great Guildhall Taylor created a building of originality and presence quite unlike the average Town Hall or Guildhall of the period.[7]

138. Guildhall, Salisbury: detail of vermiculated rustication

6. A central staircase was built and some first-floor rooms created at the end of the 19th century.
7. In *Georgian Architecture* (1993)

By an interesting coincidence, in the year the Guildhall was begun, plans were drawn up for Henry Wyndham of St. Edmund's College for a new east-facing wing at the rear of the 16th-century building there that had been modernised in the mid-18th century (see Chapter 6). It was as if Wyndham knew that one day the Council would outgrow their new Council House and would acquire as offices the building he was now extending (this is what occurred in 1927). The fact that the architect, Samuel Pepys Cockerell (1754-1827), was a former pupil of Taylor strengthens the sense of continuity. He is best known today for his Indian-style house, Sezincote, but this lay in the future (1803) and his work at Salisbury, begun in 1790, is more sober and traditional for its time (fig.139). It would be tempting to read Taylor's influence into the pair of canted bays but in fact the southern one was a mid-18th century addition and the other was put there to provide a balance (though the southern one must have been re-faced as the brickwork remains unbroken and consistent from end to end). Between them is a tripartite window of great elegance and presence that owes more to the delicacy of Adam than to the rough earthiness of Taylor.

***139**. Council House, Bourne Hill, Salisbury: east wing (Samuel Pepys Cockerell, 1788)*

A new, more extensive residence was being built in the middle of the county at about this time, Stoke Park at Erlestoke (1786-91), for which the architect was George Steuart (1730-1806). He came from Atholl in Perthshire and, apart from a house in London for the 3rd Duke of Atholl, most of his

140. *Stoke Park, Erlestoke (George Steuart, 1786-91): engraving drawn and published by J.P.Neale, 1822.*

work was in Scotland and in Shropshire,[8] his two best-known buildings being at Shrewsbury – St.Chad's Church and Attingham Park. Stoke Park House, on a hill east of the village, has been largely demolished and what remains has been incorporated into a detention centre. Only two wings remain, "with characteristically attenuated Ionic pilasters" (Pevsner). The house is illustrated in John Britton's *Beauties of Wiltshire* and in an engraving by J.P.Neale (fig.140). An elegant Doric gatehouse survives (now the prison visitors' waiting room) and, near the church, a pair of gateposts (fig.141), rusticated and topped by decorated urns. The urn on the left in the picture is made of natural stone, that on the right (a later replacement, perhaps) of Coade stone.[9] The village itself is interesting for the assortment of carvings inserted into the stonework of several of its cottages. These are of medieval or Tudor origin and probably came from the house that was demolished by its owner, Joshua Smith, to make way for the new one.

At the end of the 18th century, architectural practice was dominated by James Wyatt (1746-1813), the most prominent member of the great dynasty[10] of Wyatts that included his brother Samuel and his nephew Jeffry. James

8. Another project in southern England for which Steuart has been suggested as the architect is that part of Combe Hay Manor House, south of Bath, built in about 1770.
9. The artificial stone made by Elinor Coade and her daughter in the 18th and early 19th century. The formula and method were not passed on when the daughter died but at Lyme Regis, where Elinor Coade lived, the local museum contains (and sells) modern 'Coade stone' made on the basis of analysis carried out by the British Museum Research Laboratory.
10. Colvin includes a family tree (in his *Biographical Dictionary*) of all known (male) Wyatts descending from James's grandfather, John. There were probably more than 40 that made their living in building, architecture, the visual arts or estate management, of which at least 30 achieved distinction.

141. Gateposts at Erlestoke: one of the few survivals of Stoke Park

had shot to prominence in 1770 when, soon after returning from his Grand Tour, he entered and won a competition for a large suite of rooms in Oxford Street which were to be known as 'The Pantheon'. This success launched him into a career of designing for the rich and famous including royalty. Though a man of great personal charm, he infuriated clients through his lack of attention (brought about by taking on far too much work). But, despite a growing reputation for inefficiency, he continued, right up to his death in a coaching accident in 1813, to attract prestigious commissions and important public appointments, including the most important of all in architecture, that of Surveyor-General, upon the death of Sir William Chambers in 1796. His architectural style was eclectic. His early training was Palladian but, later in life, he confessed that, after returning from Italy, "he found the public taste corrupted by the Adams and he was obliged to comply with it". In the light of this readiness to follow fashion, it comes as no surprise that his repertoire included a highly restrained form of neo-classicism (of which Castle Coole, Co.Fermanagh is, perhaps, the finest example), Greek Revival (such as at Dodington House, Gloucestershire) and, more and more as his career progressed, Gothic (Lee Priory and Fonthill Abbey being prime examples). It is difficult to be sure whether Wyatt's Gothic should be spelt with a 'k', the form usually reserved for the fanciful, make-believe, stick-on Gothic pioneered by Horace Walpole at Strawberry Hill, Middlesex. All these 18th-century attempts at the style would later be condemned by the more serious-minded Gothic Revivalists in the 19th

142. *Hartham Park, Biddestone (James Wyatt, 1790-95): engraving from* Beauties of Wiltshire *by John Britton*

century and Wyatt would come in for more than his fair share of vilification. Yet Wyatt, alone amongst the Georgians, was starting to develop a proper feel for Gothic and some credit him with an important role in its development.

In Wiltshire, his name is probably best known in connection with two unfortunate commissions (both beyond the scope of this book): restoration work at Salisbury Cathedral for Bishop Barrington[11] and alterations at Wilton House (including the Gothic 'Cloisters') for the 11th Earl of Pembroke. But two happier engagements in the county were for country houses, at Hartham Park (1790-95) and Bowden Park (1796). Hartham Park House, near Biddestone, has been extended at each end in such a way as to alter its original simple character but the house as it was originally built features in an illustration in Volume III of John Britton's *Beauties of Wiltshire* (1825) (fig.142). Britton tells us that the house was built by James Wyatt for Lady James in a "peculiarly chaste style both of the elevations and the internal design in all respects, worthy of his acknowledged genius and science". It is a seven-bay house, with the central three bays being canted outwards. It has some vestigial Palladian features in the form of shallow, detached window heads (both triangular and elliptical), which do not appear in Britton's illustration, and a balustrade running along the top of the wall.

11. For an account of how James Wyatt's reputation was later to suffer at the hands of A.W.N.Pugin, see the article by Richard Durman, 'James Wyatt and Salisbury Cathedral, the Demonising of an Architect', in *The Hatcher Review* (Volume Five, No.43).

143. *Bowden Park House (James Wyatt, 1796)*

Bowden Park House was built for Mr.Barnard Dickinson, heir to a Jamaican fortune, and is a small masterpiece of a Greek-inspired style with a particularly graceful bowed and colonnaded southern end (fig.143). Both designs exude good taste and quality and demonstrate that, for all his faults, Wyatt had an easy, natural feel for good design that was not surpassed by any of his contemporaries.

16 The Goths are Coming – 1800 to 1835

By 1800, it is no longer just a matter of whether Palladianism was dead but of how much longer classicism itself would survive as the prevalent building style in Britain. There had already been a few isolated examples of Georgian Gothick: at Lacock Abbey, John Ivory Talbot had employed Sanderson Miller in 1753-55 to build him a new Hall, now the most prominent and characteristic feature of this National Trust property; in Bath, a chapel was built at The Vineyards, which opened in 1765, for the Countess of Huntingdon's 'Connexion', a dissenting, Calvanistic sect which built a series of similar chapels in other towns. Both of these buildings, typically for their period, contain Gothic adornments but otherwise owe little to true Gothic architecture either in spirit or structure. The same was true, of course, of the way John Nash turned the exterior of Lancelot Brown's Picture Gallery at Corsham Court into an outwardly Gothick building. It was true too of no less than four other ecclesiastical buildings in Bath (recorded by Ison) that have been demolished – St.James's Church (1768-69) by John Palmer and Thomas Jelly; Margaret Chapel, Brock Street (c.1773) by John Wood the Younger; All Saints Chapel (opened 1794) and Christ Church, Montpelier Row (opened 1798), both by John Palmer.

In 1795, James Wyatt had begun work at Fonthill for William Beckford. The 'Abbey' there, England's most famous building in its short lifetime, would reach the height of its prominence in 1801 when, though still unfinished, it received a much-publicised visit from Lord Nelson, then England's favourite hero. Superficially, this was still the romantic Gothick of Horace Walpole but, whereas Strawberry Hill was a charming diversion in the Age of Reason, at Fonthill Abbey all sense of reason or enlightenment seemed to be set aside in the face of its owner's manic self-obsession. Wyatt clearly could not resist the challenge of this unique and unprecedented commission but its sheer monstrosity would do nothing but harm both to his equanimity and his reputation. It was also in 1801 that Wyatt would begin his work at Wilton. The 'Cloisters' and the Gothic Entrance Halls on the north and east sides can be seen and judged on a visit to the House whenever it is open. Whatever their aesthetic merit – and they are probably better regarded today than by the Victorians – they are clearly 'Gothick'. The Gothick-style Market Cross in Devizes, erected in 1814, is normally attributed to Benjamin Wyatt (James's son); he certainly executed it, but Lord Sidmouth, for whom it was built, had given his instructions to James in 1813 before the fatal coach accident. James Wyatt's biographer, Anthony Dale, believes that the Cross is James's design and is therefore his last work. A more serious attempt to revive the spirit of Gothic was made in 1810 by John Pinch at St.Mary's Church, Bathwick. It takes a while to realise that it is Georgian and it foreshadows the coming Gothic Revival in remarkable and impressive fashion.[1]

Alongside these developments, the bounds of neo-classicism were being pushed further out, especially to embrace the new taste for Greek architecture. The Greek influence operated in two ways. The first was little more than a modification of basic Palladian forms. We have already seen an example of this in Bowden Park House and more would follow, as we shall see, in Pythouse, near Semley, in Philipps House, Dinton and in Devizes Town Hall. Some of the buildings of the early Palladian revival like Chiswick House and Ralph Allen's House, Bath did not eschew richness of detail, but the group of buildings just cited show that, in these late stages of classicism, the line between 'Palladian' and 'Greek' is a fine one. Both can be seen as representing plainness and simplicity – the antithesis of anything Baroque or 'unnecessarily' elaborate. And, in the hands of an architect like James Wyatt, each came to absorb the spirit of the other.

The other form of Greek influence comprised a more radical attempt to re-create or re-interpret actual buildings of ancient Greece which were becoming known to a wider public; it is this that is usually referred to as the Greek Revival. A pioneering example of Greek Revival was seen at Trafalgar Park (Revett's porch) and later examples that can still be seen in Bath are Doric House (1803) by J.M.Gandy, The Masonic Hall (now the Friends' Meeting House) of 1817-19 by William Wilkins, the pavilions at Cleveland Bridge of 1827 by H.E.Goodridge and, lastly, Partis College, also 1827, by Samuel and Philip Flood Page. One, sadly, that has gone is the Tepid Baths (1830) by the fine neo-classicist, Decimus Burton. A late example, by T.H.Wyatt (a distant relative of James) is his Assize Courts, Devizes of 1835, currently (2000) unused and officially 'at risk', though repair works are being undertaken.

None of this was to have any significant effect on the ever-spreading terraces of Bath. Neither Baldwin nor Eveleigh would practise again in Bath after their financial troubles but Palmer would remain on the scene a little longer. Other talented architects to emerge were John Pinch (1770-1827) and Charles Harcourt Masters (b.1759). All these were content or, perhaps, felt obliged to follow broadly in the stylistic footprints of their distinguished predecessors. John Pinch, a Bath builder, also suffered bankruptcy soon after 1800 but was able to continue to work as an architect and surveyor. He built up a practice which he was able to pass on to his talented son, another John. The principal legacy of the elder Pinch is a number of Regency terraces as elegant and refined as any which we have seen so far. He also designed Bishopstrow House, near Warminster,[2] also in a late Georgian classical style. John Pinch junior (died 1849), on the other hand, practised in a world firmly under the

1. Other examples of Georgian Gothic can be found at The Moat House, Britford (near Salisbury) which was refaced with pointed windows and crenellations in 1766; and at Froxfield, where the Somerset Hospital (founded 1694 and extended 1775) was given a new Gothick gateway and chapel in 1813.
2. Now a hotel and restaurant.

144. *Sion Hill Place, Bath (John Pinch I, 1817-20)*

influence of Greek and Gothic; he was responsible for the Grecian-style buildings on the west side of Queen Square that fill the gap left by John Wood the Elder and for a series of Gothic churches in Somerset and, in Wiltshire, the south aisle and porch at Crittleton (1836). Harcourt Masters (the 'Harcourt' was a late adoption), another architect and surveyor of Bath, also designed several terraces but is, perhaps, best known for Sydney Hotel (Holburne Museum) which will be described later in view of its mixed authorship.

Bath's great days as a spa town were in the past but it would remain sufficiently fashionable to justify considerable further expansion until about 1840. Its growth would now include a leap across the river to the slopes of the hills in the south as well as pushing out in the directions it had already gone. To the north, Pinch would design Cavendish Place (1805-8), Park Street (1808), Cavendish Crescent (1817-30), and Sion Hill Place (1817-20) (fig.144). At Cavendish Place we see a splendid example of Pinch's system for adapting a terrace of houses to a sloping site with its horizontal bands and cornices designed to flow from one house to the next, rather than be broken as in the system preferred by the Woods, Atwood and Palmer. The magnificent fanlights and the balconies give the terrace a distinctive 'Regency' flavour though otherwise the overall style conforms very closely to the norms established in Bath nearly 100 years previously. The refinement of the details (fig.145) mark out these terraced dwellings as homes for the discerning – suitably 'modern' but fitting in to the established Bath scene. The same was true of the terraces designed by Pinch on the east side of the city. These comprise 'New' Sydney Place (1807-08), balancing Baldwin's Sydney Place on the other side of the mouth of Great Pulteney Street where it meets Sydney Gardens; Daniel Street (1810), running behind and parallel to Baldwin's Sydney Place; and, finally, Raby Place (1825), further to the south of Sydney Gardens. The first of these is, perhaps, Pinch's masterpiece, with great overall presence and many strong and interesting features (fig.146). The general arrangement of its longest, north-facing façade is of three 3-bay pedimented pavilions separated by ranges of four 3-bay units. There is something of Northumberland Buildings about the incorporation of the attic storey as an upper floor, but here Pinch makes it an unequivocal fourth storey and places it below the pavilion pediments, a more convincing arrangement than Baldwin's of an attic sitting uncomfortably on top of three pedimented floors. The pavilions are given

145. *Cavendish Place, Bath (John Pinch I, 1805-08): detail*

146. *New Sydney Place, Bath (John Pinch I, 1807-08)*

***147** & **148**. (left) Southcot Place, Bath (perhaps by Charles Harcourt Masters, early 19th century)*
(right) Widcombe Terrace, Bath (Charles Harcourt Masters, 1805)

further presence by the framing of the first-floor central windows by pilaster strips surmounted by consoles, a decorative frieze and a straight, projecting cornice. The site has a gentle upwards slope from west to east and, as at Cavendish Place, this is handled by the 'flowing' rather than the 'stepped' method. The return façades at each end are cleverly linked to the main façade by two-bay bows and each is given further interest by a square, projecting Doric porch set in the 'area' between the building and the railings at the back of the pavement.

To the west, Nelson Street and Nile Street, by their very names, indicate development of around 1800. To the south, Lyncombe Hill and Southcot Place (fig.147) were built during this Regency period: a charming group of houses which does not get any kind of mention from Ison, such is the scale of Bath's collection of Georgian buildings. A little to the west, in Prior Park Road, are Prior Park Buildings (c.1825), which Ison attributes to the elder

Pinch. It is an unusual range for Bath, being well set back from the road and having an exceptionally plain façade (though with a rusticated ground floor) and three windows, including a central oval one, in the huge tympanum of the central pediment. Moving a little more to the west we come to Widcombe Crescent and Widcombe Terrace (1805) by Harcourt Masters (fig.148) built to make the best of the views to the rear. Allowing for this, they are another well-mannered and elegant development but do not compare favourably with Pinch's achievements. An interesting feature of the Crescent is that as well as curving in plan it dips slightly to each side in elevation, with three downward breaks on each side. The plat bands at these six points are stepped but the cornice has been designed to 'flow' in the system used by Pinch (and now to become a regular feature of even the meanest Bath terraces).

In parallel with these urban terrace developments a new form of sub-urban housing was being pioneered by H.E.Goodridge, whose contribution to the buildings of Bath is considerable. He is best known, perhaps for Cleveland Bridge (where his name can be read by thousands of motorists each day waiting in the heavy traffic queues it now bears), for Lansdown Tower ('Beckford's Tower') as well as for The Corridor, High Street and chapels in Argyle Street (the façade) and Charlotte Street. The Bazaar, Quiet Street and the Argyll and Royal Hotels, Manvers Street (c.1840) are also attributed to him. All of these (with the exception of the former Percy Chapel, Charlotte Street) are mainly Greek-inspired. But he also later designed and built a series of villas, in an Italianate style, that would establish a pattern for Bath's detached houses, for which there was now a greater demand.

Another individual building that was added to Bath's collection in late Georgian times was the Theatre Royal. It is possible to visit the theatre of this name without being aware of the existence of the Georgian façade in Beaufort Square which originally contained the entrance. After a fire in the 19th century the entrance was switched to the Sawclose end, the former house of Beau Nash incorporated into it and the plump, welcoming foyer added. The designer of the original building was George Dance the Younger (1741-1825), appointed in 1805. His authorship, with Sir Robert Taylor, of the London Building Act 1774, demonstrating his high standing in the profession, has already been noted. However, it was as an innovative designer that he had proved himself from an early age and, though he was to be outshone in his lifetime by more energetic and ambitious men, his work would prove to be inspirational to the next generation, especially John Smirke and his pupil John Soane. At All Hallows Church, London Wall (1765-7), he used an order without an entablature more reminiscent of the early Renaissance and a form of vaulting that anticipated Soane. Two contrasting buildings (of which neither now exist), both showing great originality and imagination, were Newgate Prison and the Council Chamber at London's Guildhall. His approach to classical design, not unlike some of his French contemporaries,

149. *Theatre Royal, Bath: the original entrance front (George Dance the Younger, begun 1805)*

was to give more attention to the geometric shapes than the niceties of classical details. All this may come as a surprise when confronted with the masks and festoons and other enrichment that bedeck what now appears to be the flank frontage of the theatre (fig.149) but, strip all these away, and simple strong lines remain. This was a late work for Dance, 30 years or more after his pioneering days, and it may be he did little more than send down a design which John Palmer executed; at any rate, Palmer, according to Ison, later tried to take most of the credit for it.[3] An important part of the internal decoration was a series of ceiling paintings donated by Paul Methuen of Corsham Court.

An interesting piece of classical building endeavour of the early 19th century in Wiltshire is Pythouse, Newtown, near Semley, also referred to as 'The Pythouse' or 'Pyt House'. An older house had stood here, in the ownership of the Benett family and in 1805 it was partly rebuilt and extended by its owner, John Benett (1773-1852), nick-named 'Long John', to his own design:

> Mr.Benett ... arranged his own plans and supervised the execution of them from the beginning to its completion, rising at 5 o'clock every morning for that purpose.[4]

3. Neil Jackson (in *Nineteenth Century Bath*) doubts if Palmer had anything to do with the building and suggests there has been some confusion with the John Palmer who developed the mail coach services and who was the lessee of the Theatre Royal.
4. This, says Colvin, is according to some contemporary MS. notes on the 'District around Shaftesbury'.

150. *Pythouse, near Semley (John Benett, 1805)*

His father, too, had apparently been an amateur architect as the top stage of nearby Tisbury church is attributed to him. The house is in a severe neo-classical style (fig.150). The tetrastyle detached Ionic portico is in the Greek style with tight, flat volutes instead of volutes projecting at 45 degrees which (despite the elder Wood's admiration of the similar Roman style used, by Inigo Jones as he supposed, in Bath's Old Guildhall) was the normal usage in England (including by Wood). The recessed bay with columns, on each side of the building, is, again, a feature inspired by Greek architecture rather than Roman. Inside there is an unusual iron staircase, designed by Benett, that rises from the centre of a long, narrow central hall then divides and rises again in two flights in the opposite direction (fig.151). In the grounds is an attractive Orangery that is older than the house and is claimed to be by Lancelot

151. *Pythouse: the staircase*

Brown (in the property leaflet) though neither Pevsner nor Colvin mention this attribution and its origin appears obscure.

It would appear that John Benett's activities were being noted with some care by a neighbour and distant relative, in Dinton, a few miles away. This was William Wyndham, the fourth of that name to live at Dinton and whose ancestor Sir John Wyndham had come from the Felbrigg (Norfolk) branch of the extensive Wyndham family. (Henry Wyndham of Salisbury was of another branch.[5]) Soon after Benett had completed his re-styled Pythouse, William Wyndham engaged the architect Jeffry Wyatt to undertake a similar modernisation of his old house at Dinton but he was later persuaded by Wyatt that it would be better to start again and work began on a new house in 1813 and was completed in 1816. In 1917, the estate was acquired by Bertram Philipps and the property has been known as 'Philipps House' since that time. Jeffry Wyatt (1766-1840) was a nephew of James Wyatt and had been a pupil first of Samuel and later James himself. His career reflects the increasing turmoil in which architectural practise was finding itself. He could, as here and, as we shall see, at Claverton, design in a competent classical manner but most of his work would be in Gothic or 'Tudor collegiate'. He had not long finished work at Longleat where he had undertaken many internal alterations (including the impressive staircase) and had built the stables in a style to match the house. Between 1824 and 1837, he worked at Windsor Castle and was largely responsible for giving Windsor its present outward appearance by rebuilding or extending the existing Norman and medieval towers. It was here, in 1827, that he applied to his client and sovereign, George IV, to be permitted to call himself 'Wyatville', it being fashionable at the time to make such an addition to one's name for extra grandeur. The King is reputed to have replied "Ville or mutton, call yourself what you like". In the following year, he was knighted, thus becoming, surprisingly, the first architect (except Wren, of course) whose work features in this book to be so honoured for his architectural services. (The only other would be Sir John Soane; Chamber's knighthood was Swedish and Taylor's was for services to the City of London).

A feature of Philipps House that marks it out from what we have seen before is the assymetry of its layout, with a stable and service block to one side – an aggressively non-Palladian arrangement pioneered, and made respectable, by James Wyatt at Dodington House. But its other remarkable feature is its similarity to Pythouse, not only in its architectural style (figs.152 & 153) but in its setting, both houses being sited on a south-facing hillside with trees along the ridge behind and pasture land below.[6]

5. This is how both Salisbury and Dinton come to have a *Wyndham Arms* pub – one on land once part of Henry Wyndham's estate and the other re-named in 1998 after the Wyndhams of Dinton.
6. Despite these similarities, Giles Worsley suggests, in *Architectural Drawings of the Regency Period* (Andre Deutsch, 1991) that Wyatt drew on the design for Woodfold Hall, Lancashire on which he had worked while still in his uncle's office; and, in a paper published in vol.141 of the *Transactions of the Somerset Archaeology and Natural History Society*, William Evans presents a strong case for Leigh Court, North Somerset, being based by its architect, Thomas Hopper, on Pythouse.

152 & 153. *(left) Pythouse (right) Philipps House*

Outside, the building is in a severely plain neo-classical style, typical of its time and still loosely Palladian. But, in a way that Palladio, Inigo Jones or Lord Burlington would find puzzling, the restraint and severity are continued inside as well. It is true that it contains some plaster frieze ornaments that look forward to the sort of floral decoration that the Victorians would love, but their presence remains discreet. The glory of the house is the central hall and its staircase, top lit by a circular dome (fig.154). It is difficult to imagine a more impressive blend of grandeur and austerity.

Wyatt (as he still was) would soon be working in the (Bristol) Avon valley just east of Bath, building a new manor house, Claverton Manor (1819-20) for John Vivian. With its two massive bays facing across the valley it is a noble presence standing high above the road, railway and canal beneath. Between the bows are an elegant porch and two attached giant Ionic columns.[7]

7. Perhaps a more typical work of Wyatville was the vast, gothic, castellated Rood Ashton, at West Ashton, now partly restored, and the remainder demolished, after lying in ruins for many years.

154. *Philipps House: central staircase. (The National Trust)*

Between the time of these two ventures by Jeffry Wyatt, Thomas Baldwin made a re-appearance, as architect of a new Town Hall for Devizes, which felt that it had outgrown the one by Lawrence. Both Bath and Salisbury had fine Town Halls and now Devizes would join them. The new building, erected 1806-08 (fig.155), though not large, entirely fills an island site at the head of the lane leading to St.John's Church. Baldwin, therefore, needed to apply the skill he had shown at Bath in making the rear of the building a feature in its own right. He achieved this here by giving the service end of the building a smooth stone-clad curve with a minimum of window space (fig.156). The formal western end consists of a rusticated ground floor and a taller first floor with a giant engaged Ionic order topped by a plain frieze and parapet. Three of its five bays form a bow, rising through the entire building. The contrasting arrangement and design of the windows in each floor is unusual and effective. There is hint of the Greek in the Ionic capitals and the spareness of the frieze but the Palladian predominates. It is a design that does credit to the town as well as to a man whose days in Bath had been ended in such sad and premature fashion.[8] "A fine, elegant, accomplished little building", says Pevsner. Indeed.

8. A late-Georgian house in Wiltshire attributed to Baldwin is Rainscombe House, Oare.

155. *Town Hall, Devizes (Thomas Baldwin, 1806-08): west front*

156. *Town Hall, Devizes from the south-east*

157. *Amesbury Abbey (John Webb, 1661): engraving from* Beauties of Wiltshire *by John Britton.*

To close this chapter, we need to return to two of the country houses that appeared much earlier – Tottenham House and Amesbury Abbey – for both received drastic facelifts at the very end of the classical era. Tottenham House was now held by Charles Brudenell-Bruce, 1st Marquis of Ailesbury (whose father had married Henry Hoare's daughter, Susanna). As if to demonstrate that Palladianism was in his veins, he spent a larger sum than he could comfortably afford to enlarge Burlington's villa and employed Thomas Cundy (1765-1825) as his architect. Cundy's first post had been clerk of works to S.P.Cockerell and he later became surveyor to Lord Grosvenor's London estates. He designed, according to Colvin, "in either picturesque Gothic style reminiscent of Nash, or else in a conventional classical manner calculated to appeal to patrons who disliked the deviations of Dance or Soane". Cundy died during the work (1823-26) and it was executed by his eldest son Thomas. The original villa was not demolished but it was entirely swamped by the new Palladian building and few traces of it now remain. Amesbury Abbey, where John Webb had built a Palladian house for the 2nd Duke of Somerset in 1661, had, by the 19th century, come into the possession of the Antrobus family and, in 1834, Thomas Hopper (1776-1856) was engaged by Sir Edmund Antrobus to enlarge and modernise it. Now, we have already seen a certain pragmatic flexibility in the work of, for example, James Wyatt, his nephew Jeffry and, to an extent, John Pinch. In 1830, Thomas Hopper had gone on record as saying: "It is the business of an architect to understand all styles, and to be prejudiced in favour of none". He practised what he preached, designing in Palladian, Greek Doric, Greek Ionic, Tudor Gothic, Jacobethan, Norman, Gothic and Egyptian. He had already built the extraordinary Norman Revival Penrhyn Castle, Gwynedd

158. Amesbury Abbey (Thomas Hopper, begun 1834)

for the slate magnate G.H.Dawkins Pennant and now he turned his attention to the enlargement of a Palladian villa. He did so with great gusto and ingenuity and what we see today, though very different from the original, incorporates some of its fabric and a great deal of its Palladian spirit (figs.157 & 158). The tetrastyle giant portico has become hexastyle and more imposingly regal. It is now supported by a large *porte-cochère* and extends the full height of an extended façade. This retains Webb's rusticated ground and first floors but now contains a full second floor with windows strongly marked by decorative features above them. A central tower, providing light to a massive stone staircase inside, replaces the belvedere. As if this was not enough, each side is embellished by a giant engaged portico (Composite, as at the front) incorporating an attic and topped by decorative urns (fig.159). This is Palladianism going out with a bang.

159. Amesbury Abbey: east side (detail)

17 The Georgian Inheritance

Nearly all that has gone before are buildings of some prestige – either in the public domain or else mansions or villas for the landed classes or, at the least, second or seasonal homes in Bath for the well-to-do with principal homes in London or on their own estates. But, as the 18th century progressed, more people of moderate means came to live in Bath's new terraces and, in general, with a growing middle class and with increasing urbanisation, the desire for good design in buildings became more widespread. We have seen the influence of the pattern book in helping to establish standards and design details that have led to the good manners and consistency that we associate with Georgian architecture. 'Architecture' for the accommodation of the lower classes took a little longer. John Wood's cottages for Ralph Allen's workers are a rare and early example. Normally, it was not an aspect of building in which any ambitious architect would have the slightest interest.

One who did was John Wood the Younger. In 1780, he decided to find out for himself the conditions in which the common labourer and their families lived and he was moved and shocked by what he saw – tumbledown cottages that were damp, insanitary and crowded. The architect of the Royal Crescent and Bath's Assembly Rooms set about writing *A Series of Plans for Cottages or Habitations of the Labourer* which was published in 1781. The book was intended as a building guide – to any landowner or employer who was prepared to take any notice of it – and contained a great variety of simple plans for small dwellings that would provide decent, sound accommodation for the tenant at minimum expenditure to the owner.[1] However, it was not until the 1860s that the work of a Royal Commission finally made the nation aware of the scandal that existed and many more years were to follow before serious improvements were made. We must assume that Wood's book became no more than an unusual addition to the country house library. The great majority of surviving workers' terraces of the Georgian era are from the late 18th or early 19th centuries. Any older ones would have been so inadequate that they would have been demolished long ago. A few built for workers in the woollen trade can be found in Bradford-on-Avon, probably from the middle of the century.

For most towns in England, any growth in the 18th century was piecemeal and limited. Bath was the most extreme exception, bursting its medieval seams very early in the 18th century and rolling on outwards in all directions for more than a hundred years (before joining in the more general growth of the 19th and 20th centuries). Only in Bathwick was there any sort of

1. Several of these are illustrated in *Life in the English Country Cottage* by Adrian Tinniswood (Weidenfeld & Nicolson, London, 1995).

formal plan being followed but, on the other hand, the exciting progression from Queen Square to the Circus and on through Brock Street to the Royal Crescent cannot have depended entirely upon land acquisitions and luck. We shall be able to understand more about the way towns in Wiltshire may have developed at this time when a study (due for completion in 2001) by Wiltshire County Council Archaeological Service is published. However, it is likely that any physical growth that could be called significant was limited to the woollen industrial towns of West Wiltshire, especially Bradford-on-Avon. Other towns were certainly active and prosperous and there was a great deal of new development but it was largely in the nature of rebuilding, re-furbishment or what we would now call 'infill'. At Devizes, for example, there was quite an upsurge of activity, with new houses being built and many more receiving a Georgian face-lift, but it amounted to little more than a further bout of consolidation of the town within the medieval framework that had been established by the castle; Long Street may have become a little longer, and a few large houses were built on the periphery, but the street pattern did not significantly change. The same sort of thing could be said of Chippenham for all the prosperity it was enjoying at the time. In Salisbury, nearly all Georgian development was contained within the medieval core – the Chequers and the Cathedral Close. Just a few new sites were developed around the fringes, in Fisherton Anger, in Milford and in Castle Street (north of the medieval gate). Cricklade confined itself to the square plan of its town walls and Wootton Bassett contained any new development within the burgage plots along its main street. Even Marlborough, a town that prospered through the coaching trade in Georgian times, confined all new building in this period to the ancient structure of the town; one reason for this was that it had suffered a disastrous fire in 1653 (followed by others in 1679 and 1690) from which it took a long time to recover. Calne at that time was little more than a village and significant growth did not come till later. Corsham had some modest growth at the south end of its High Street and Malmesbury pushed out a little in the only direction it was able because of its particular topography, namely, to the north-west. One town, apart from Bradford, that did show some growth was Trowbridge – mainly in and around The Halve – and this continued into the Regency period. And, in 1814, Melksham experienced a spa boom. But it was short-lived and only a few Regency-style houses in Spa Road survive as a reminder.

Within these towns, it is possible to trace the architectural trends that have been exemplified in earlier chapters by 'grander' examples. Provincial Baroque abounds in Devizes and examples can be found in other towns, especially Salisbury. Then, as Palladian principles became more widespread, we see more subdued examples of mid-Georgian classicism, especially in Warminster, Marlborough and Bradford-on-Avon. The typical mid-Georgian house with large plain windows and ornate doorways can be found throughout the county. Some, where it could be afforded, have one or more

***160**. A fine pair of mid-18th-century houses: Nos.10 and 11 Kingsbury Street, Marlborough*

***161**. No.47 Endless Street, Salisbury (1830): showing the influence of George Dance*

Venetian windows (fig.160). However, it is, perhaps, more accurate to say that the typical 'Georgian' house is more a reversion to 'Puritan Minimalism' than an adaptation of Palladianism. On this view, and accepting that it was the hand of Inigo Jones in the post-Restoration house, Jones's influence on the buildings of Britain becomes more immense than ever. For good Regency examples it is necessary to go to Bath, though even there there is nothing to be found in quite the same vein as in Brighton or Cheltenham. An isolated example of a more typical Regency house is No.11 Long Street, Devizes. A few more of this

162. Houses in Southbroom Road, Devizes (early 19th century): showing the influence of Sir John Soane

period can be found in Spa Road in Melksham which, in 1814, tried, with little success, to emulate Bath as a spa town. Salisbury has an interesting example of a late classical house (now an office) at No.47 Endless Street (fig.161); this is from 1830 and shares the simplified approach to classical design shown by George Dance. And, in Southbroom Road, Devizes, can be found a short row of houses of a classical simplicity that excels even Soane (fig.162).

A widespread practice throughout the Georgian era was to alter existing buildings to give them a fashionable Georgian appearance. This was achieved by creating a new façade in the form of an outer skin, of stone or brick, with appropriate changes to the fenestration and the addition of suitable details like window frames and door cases. The process was usually so skilfully done that the existence of an older building behind the Georgian face is difficult to detect. Iford Manor (between Bath and Bradford-on-Avon) is an example of a large country house that has been so treated but it was a common practice in the towns. Devizes, for example, has many buildings in and around its Market Place which were given a modern façade in the 18th century disguising their true age. In Salisbury, the surface skin sometimes consisted of mathematical tiles fixed to battens covering the wall behind. A mathematical tile is one with an exposed surface of the same size and shape of the outward face of a building brick and designed to interlock with its neighbours in such a fashion as to give a false impression of normal brickwork (fig.163). This system, cheaper and lighter than a skin of real brick, can be found extensively in Kent and Sussex but very little elsewhere in the rest of

***163**. Mathematical tiles*

Britain – except in Salisbury.[2] One possible reason for this is that this form of tiling is particularly well suited to disguising timber-framed buildings (as brick-built Georgian ones) and Salisbury – like the south-east of the country – had a great number of these.

Two interesting examples can be found in St.Ann's Street. The dark red mathematical tiles covering the St. Ann's Street façade of Windover House disguise a building from about 1600. A more dramatic use of the system can be seen a few doors away at Nos.36/38 (fig.164), two houses that were combined and 'modernised' in the 18th century with a new central doorcase and a skin of mathematical tiles which, on this occasion, were of a yellowy/grey colour made of gault clay (often referred to as 'white' brick). But these houses date from the 15th century and had been built with the first floor 'jettied' over the ground floor in the characteristic manner of the period. The jetty was retained with rather bizarre (if charming) results, heightened by the classical consoles fixed beneath the overhang. (Another example of a jettied building given a Georgian facelift, this time in render, can be seen in the house next to the Swan Hotel, Church Street, Bradford-on-Avon.) At No.47 Winchester Street, Salisbury, the appearance of the principal façade as a Georgian house is given away as a deceit by the contrasting 'old-fashioned' 17th-century brickwork on the return façade in St.Edmund's Church Street (fig.165). A few examples of mathematical tiles are also found in Marlborough.

This 'Georgianisation' of buildings was especially popular for inns. Almost every country or village inn in Wiltshire of the 17th century or earlier seems to have been modernised in Georgian times, if only by the substitution of sash windows for mullions, often with an enlargement at the same time. A few random examples are the New Inn, Amesbury; the Queen's Head, Broadchalke; the Cross Keys, Fovant; and the George, Shrewton. In Downton, the Bull, the Queen's Head and the White Horse have all been

2. Rare examples can be found as far west as Bideford in Devon and as far north as Althorp House, Northamptonshire, where, on the advice of Henry Holland who found the original brickwork "too hot", the house was entirely covered in yellow tiles nailed directly to the existing bricks.

164. *Nos.36-38 St.Ann's Street, Salisbury: two 15th-century houses*

dressed in Georgian clothes to appear younger than they are, in contrast to the Wooden Spoon which was actually newly-built in the 18th century. The practice of 'modernising' windows even extended to medieval buildings. During the time that the former 14th-century chapel over St.Ann's Gate in Salisbury Cathedral Close was in the ownership of the Harris family, its three Gothic windows were replaced by Georgian-style sash windows. The existing Gothic-style windows date from about 1909.[3]

3. RCHM Report, *City of Salisbury*, Vol.I.

165. *No.47 Winchester Street, Salisbury: Georgian tiled front on a 17th-century building*

166. *The White Hart Hotel, St.John Street, Salisbury (c.1820)*

The Georgian period also excelled in coaching inns. A particularly grand example is the White Hart Hotel, Salisbury (c.1820), with its magnificent Ionic portico above an arched support projecting into the street (fig.166). Another elegant example is the Pembroke Arms Hotel in neighbouring Wilton (fig.167). It gives every impression of being a purpose-built hotel but the DoE list states that it is possibly by James Wyatt and was apparently used to house some of the workforce engaged on his alterations to Wilton House. Other prominent (predominantly) 18th-century inns are the Antrobus Arms at Amesbury; the Bear Hotel and the Black Swan at Devizes; the Swan Hotel at Bradford-on-

167. *The Pembroke Arms Hotel, Wilton (attributed to James Wyatt, c.1801)*

168. The Swan Hotel, Bradford-on-Avon (mid-18th century): to the right the Georgianisation of an earlier jettied building

Avon (fig.168); the Old Bell Inn at Warminster; the Castle and Ball and the Ailesbury Arms Hotel at Marlborough; and the Grosvenor Arms Hotel at Hindon (fig.169). Even Swindon has managed to retain its Georgian coaching inn, the Goddard Arms in the High Street.

A town, apart from fashionable Bath, to be graced with Assembly Rooms was Salisbury – in 1802, on a site at the corner of High Street and New Canal, now Waterstone's bookshop (and for many years W.H.Smith, whose name appears on the delightful little clocktower and weather vane added in about 1925). Its three long, round-topped windows were even longer originally and below them, in the High Street, once stood a Doric porch at which visitors' carriages could halt.

169. Grosvenor Arms Hotel, Hindon: a reminder of Hindon's importance in Georgian coaching days

170. *Old Town Hall, Westbury (1815)*

Town Halls in a classical style – in addition to those already noted at Devizes (two of them), Bath and Salisbury – can be found at Westbury (1815) (fig.170) and Corsham (1784 with 1882 additions) and a charming Market House of 1835 can be found at Devizes. Wootton Bassett's best-known feature, its Town Hall, raised on primitive Doric columns, dates from 1700 but with its ornate timbering is more 'quaint' than 'classical'. A former Town Hall that time has treated badly is in the Market Place at Wilton. It began life in 1737 as a dignified presence in the heart of the town but, in 1889, the Victorians turned it into a Town Hall more suitable for Trumpton by adding a huge clock tower to the roof. It is now submerged by traffic and by signs and other paraphernalia.

Apart from Bath, there were gaols at Salisbury, Marlborough and Devizes. Devizes, indeed, had the largest gaol of them all for a time after it was first extended, and later rebuilt on another site. It opened in 1817, and by 1868 was Wiltshire's only county gaol, but was never completed to its original, larger, plan. Both have long gone (though the original one is commemorated in the name Bridewell Street). In Salisbury, even after its Infirmary had opened in 1771, the adjoining County Gaol, on the west bank of the river Avon, was extended, first, by 24 cells (in three storeys) in 1783 and again in c.1792 by 20 cells. All that now remains, following its removal to another site early in the 19th century, is a small stone building (probably used for a time as a lock-up) which supports a Victorian clock tower. But embedded in the western wall is an interesting reminder of the large Georgian building that once stood here, a carving of shackles that would probably once have stood over its doorway (fig.171). This seems to have been a favourite decorative device, if 'decorative' is the right word, for Georgian prisons; it probably derived from Dance's Newgate Prison (1770-85) and a similar device can be seen in the Gaol at King's Lynn, Norfolk. Other towns and villages made do with a local lock-up (or 'blind-house'). Several of these built in Wiltshire in the Georgian period have survived, that at Trowbridge (fig.172) being a good example.

171. Shackles carved on the remains of the County Gaol, Fisherton Street, Salisbury (1783)

Only Bath and Hardenhuish have Georgian churches[4] but many Wiltshire towns and villages have non-conformist chapels from the period. Bath, Bradford-on-Avon and Trowbridge each have several examples and, in the villages, the Moravian Chapel (1745) at East Tytherton and the Providence Chapel (1777) at Lyneham are both worthy of note.

Above all, it is the volume and, within a polite consistency, the variety of Georgian houses that impress, not only in Bath but in nearly every town in Wiltshire, except, perhaps Swindon, which was never very large before Brunel

172. Lock-up by Town Bridge, Trowbridge (1758)

4. Though Farley has its 17th-century classical church, possibly by Wren (see Chapter 6).

***173**. Thatched Georgian cottage, Downton*

brought the railway to it in 1840 and has since lost much of its Old Town to re-development. The best of what remains is in Wood Street, High Street and Cricklade Street, No.42 being "the best house in Swindon by far" (Pevsner). In Salisbury, one should not miss St Ann's Street, New Street, Brown Street or Endless Street. The houses of The Close include a few from Georgian times but the best are earlier, as we saw in Chapter 6. In Devizes, the best of the 18th-century architecture is readily found in its Market Place and surrounding streets within the great bow of the former castle bailey, the most notable being Long Street. Marlborough, because of its disastrous 17th-century fires, has a predominantly Georgian appearance, the best examples being found in the High Street (look out for Wykeham House and the Ivy House Hotel) and the area around Kingsbury Street and The Green. Warminster has good Georgian buildings all along its principal length of Market Place, High Street, George Street and Church Street, but also worthy of exploration are Portway, Vicarage Street and Emwell Street. The best of Bradford-on-Avon's Georgian heritage lies in Church Street, Silver Street and Woolley Street, though it is a town that repays more thorough exploration. Similarly, Trowbridge has far more to offer, in terms of interesting buildings, than Fore Street mentioned in Chapter 6. At first it seems rather more forbidding than its Wiltshire neighbours since it retains the industrial character that it first took on in the 18th century, as textile mills took over from domestic working, but a stroll around (ideally with Pevsner and a street map) yields many interesting gems.

174. Compton Park, Compton Chamberlayne: the Georgian east face of a manor house from the 15th century

Of the smaller towns, Highworth has a good collection of Georgian buildings, mainly in High Street ('Inigo House' being exceptionally fine), Lechlade Street and Cricklade Road. Cricklade has a number of good 18th-century houses and Wootton Bassett is also worth a visit. Parts of Downton have an 18th-century flavour, having continued to prosper in Georgian times after its early settlement by the Bishop of Winchester in the 13th century. Hindon, another former ancient Borough, thrived during the coaching era but declined from 1831. Its predominantly Georgian character derives from the fact that it was all but destroyed in a fire in 1754. Of the 14 inns and public houses it had at that time, only The Lamb and the Goddard Arms remain.

Good examples of Georgian architecture can be found throughout Wiltshire's villages and its countryside. Indeed, there must be few villages that do not have several cottages from the Georgian period, some of them attractively thatched (fig.173), and at least one 'big' Georgian house, either its traditional manor house (fig.174) or one built by a wealthy resident. Clyffe Hall, Market Lavington (1732) is a particularly grand example with giant Corinthian columns extending through three storeys and with a three-bay pediment. Another is Oare House, a fine brick building of about 1740, which can be glimpsed at the end of its avenue of trees. There are likely to be at least one or two farmhouses nearby, either built or improved during the same period, perhaps even sporting one or more Venetian windows. A village that has more than its fair share of good 18th-century houses is Seend which attracted wealthy residents from towns like Devizes, Trowbridge and Melksham.

18 The Classical Tradition – 1835 to 2000

The words and works of Thomas Hopper observed at the end of Chapter 16 reflect a new architectural age – one in which revivals of different styles are brought out in bewildering variety like a fancy-dress parade. The one that would predominate as the 19th century went on was Gothic, not just for churches but for public buildings like law courts and town halls and even for dwellings, for rich and poor alike. This revival of Gothic was stronger in Britain than in other countries but, even here, it was never the universal style that classicism had been for 200 years or more. Classicism itself survived, initially through the work of C.P.Cockerell and others, and there were many other competing styles that came and went. For example, during the 1840s, Lombardic Romanesque became all the rage for churches which is how Wilton's remarkable parish church (1841-5) came to be built in that style.[1] If Sidney Herbert had commissioned the church ten years later, the architect, T.H.Wyatt, would no doubt have adopted the Gothic style that he would be using for his many churches throughout the Salisbury diocese. A turning point in the fortunes of Gothic nationally had been the decision to rebuild the Palace of Westminster in Perpendicular Gothic; but Sir Charles Barry who designed it was never much of a Gothicist and was afterwards better known for his versions of Renaissance architecture. It was his collaborator in the Westminster enterprise, A.W.N.Pugin, who had been responsible for the Gothic details and would turn Gothicism into a personal crusade.

At the same time, other forces were at work which very few architects at the time even recognised as being relevant to architecture – the great engineering achievements of Telford, Brunel and others and the revolutionary use of iron and glass culminating in the Crystal Palace in 1851. One architect who did was Sir Matthew Digby Wyatt, the elder brother of T.H.Wyatt, who had acted as secretary of the Great Exhibition and also as Brunel's architect for the buildings for the Great Western Railway. Ruskin may have called the Crystal Palace "a cucumber frame" but Wyatt forecast that the union of iron and glass would hail "a new era in architecture".

But it was mainly in America and Germany that the Modern Movement grew and very little modern architecture appeared in Britain until after 1945. Indeed, Britain's principal contribution to the age of technology, so far as architecture and design were concerned, was to foster the hope that it would all go away. This at any rate, could be read into the Arts and Crafts Movement and the work of architects like Shaw, Mackintosh, Voysey and, even, Lutyens. During the remainder of the 19th century and even up to World War II, all architects were capable of working in the classical idiom even if many did

1. Another that did is the former Moravian Church, Charlotte Street, Bath (1845).

175. The former Green Park station, Bath (J.H.Sanders, 1869)

not do so. But once modernism held sway, there was little call for such skills. Not only were all derivative styles regarded as reactionary but the predominant mood was that decorative enrichment was *ipso facto* bad and unnecessary. It has only been in more recent times that a saner and more balanced view has prevailed. Also, the last 25 to 30 years has seen a massive upsurge in public interest in the protection and enjoyment of Britain's architectural heritage with a corresponding increase in relevant skills.

Returning to the 19th century, a fine early example of a building in the Palladian style, conceived in the age of the Gothic (and every other) Revival, is, curiously, a railway station – Green Park station in Bath (now a shopping mall), built in 1869 (fig.175). The architect was J.H.Sanders who succeeded here in applying Palladian symmetry and calmness to the railway age with authority and competence. It is good to see that the necessary craft skills were also still alive and well.

The railway age had also produced another very different style of classical façade in Salisbury for the building (completed in 1859) that contained a Market House and a terminus (with a turntable) for the trains that used the private railway line connecting the Market Place to the main line a quarter of a mile to the west. The design was by the Engineer of the London and South East Railway Company and its clean classical lines with three massive arches and a central pediment, all in stone, remain an asset to the Market Place even though the last train ran more than 60 years ago and the Market House ceased to function not long afterwards. In 1971-72, the structure behind the façade was rebuilt to provide a new site for the public library.

176. Victoria Art Gallery, Bridge Street, Bath (J.M.Brydon, 1898): the Wilton House window (fig.27) adapted to Imperial needs

The 19th-century extensions to Bath's Guildhall have already been noted. These were by J.M.Brydon who designed the extensions to north and south in 1891 and the Library and Art Gallery, round the corner in Bridge Street, in 1898. With the increasing demands on municipalities in the late 19th century, it was inevitable that extensions would be needed. What Brydon did was to treat Baldwin's building as the central feature of a much longer one. The style of the extensions are sympathetic enough to the original, except for the towers at the ends (which seem to be loosely based on the upper half of the church of Santa Maria della Salute in Venice with its giant scrolls and dome) and which are an early example of that lumpy, energetic style often called Edwardian Baroque. Brydon also added a dome to the original building, thus giving the centre of the new composition some extra weight. The new Library and Art Gallery (now an art gallery only) had been loyally dedicated to Queen Victoria and her statue appears high up in a niche within a blind Venetian window on the outside wall. Beneath it is the subscription 'HIM VICTORIA'[2] and above it is a pediment with reclining figures and a cartouche-of-arms rising into the cornice of the building. This ensemble is clearly based on the central feature of the south front of Wilton House. But now the allusion is not to Imperial Rome or to Renaissance Italy but to Imperial Britain for both of the reclining figures are of Britannia (fig.176). It was also Brydon who added, next to the Great Pump Room, the Palladian building that now forms the entrance to the Roman Baths (1897).

2. 'Her Imperial Majesty' – a reference to the title Empress of India bestowed on her at Disraeli's insistence in 1877.

A few years later, in Salisbury, one of its most satisfying buildings was completed in 1901 – a bank[3] for the Wilts and Dorset Bank (now Lloyds TSB) (fig.177). It is unmistakeably Edwardian and enthusiastically Baroque. A balanced but rich composition is complemented by first-class execution and an interesting choice of materials – a deep golden stone from Ham Hill in Somerset on a base of Cornish granite. In earlier times, the automatic choice of stone in Salisbury would have been that from the Tisbury/Chilmark area, but, by the late 19th century, all the various quarries that had been used for the building of the Cathedral and its subsequent maintenance (including Gilbert Scott's restoration of the 1860s), were virtually spent and Ham Hill stone was used for a number of Salisbury buildings at this time.

177. Lloyds TSB building, Castle Street, Salisbury (1901): Edwardian Baroque

One of Bath's most charming buildings is the Holburne Museum in Sydney Gardens (fig.178). For visitors coming into Bath on the A36 from the east, the sight of this building, as the last corner of Sydney Place is turned and Great Pulteney Street comes into view, is a delightful introduction to the city. Not that it is at all typical of Bath's architecture and it has the provenance of a mongrel. It was conceived by Baldwin as part of his Bathwick development, as a hotel, to close the view down Great Pulteney Street, but his design (loosely based on that of The Guildhall) was taken over and altered by Harcourt Masters when he became responsible for the development of Sydney Gardens and work began in 1796. It was extended

3. The building is actually subsidiary to the (architecturally less impressive) main bank building facing the Market Place at the other end of a long L-shaped site. It is currently (2000) surplus to the bank's requirements and is to let.

178. Holburne Museum, Sydney Gardens, Bath (originally 1796: Baldwin, Harcourt Masters, Pinch and Sir Reginald Blomfield have all contributed to its present appearance)

and altered by John Pinch the Younger in 1836 and finally, and most importantly, after it had been acquired for its present museum use in 1915, it received a complete face-lift (and was re-arranged internally) by Sir Reginald Blomfield. It is Palladian in concept but the quality of its details does not stand the same scrutiny as that of anything by the Woods or Baldwin for example.

The classical tradition in Bath continued strongly into the 20th century: the number and quality of its 20th-century classical buildings is exceptional and would repay special study. To pick just one example, in 1927, Bath's Head Post Office was opened, built to an anonymous, but competent, Government Department design paying proper respect to the spirit of the place. It is sited on a wedge-shaped site at the east end of New Bond Street. Its flank façades are unexciting but the placement and design of the entrance front is a fine contribution to the street scene at this point (fig.179). It is specially fitting that the design should reflect the taste of Bath in the early 18th century since this was when two Bath residents, Ralph Allen and John Palmer (not the architect of the same name), were doing so much to develop the country's postal services and both are duly commemorated in a plaque within the circular entrance to the building.

Local government buildings, especially in big cities, had, in late-Victorian and Edwardian times, reached the heights of architectural over-statement in the name of civic pride. By the 1920s and '30s they had become more subdued and thus we find that when Wiltshire County Council came to build its headquarters building in Trowbridge, just before the war, the style

***179**. Head Post Office, New Bond Street, Bath (1927)*

is broadly Palladian and the mood imposing without being in any way showy (fig.180). The architect was P.D.Hepworth.

***180**. County Hall, Bythesea Road, Trowbridge (P.D.Hepworth, 1938-40)*

***181**. West Walk House, The Close, Salisbury (Robert Adam, 1983). (Robert Adam)*

As for the post-war period, it is only in the last 20 years or so that any serious attempt to recapture the Palladian spirit is likely to be found. A notable example is to be found in Salisbury Cathedral Close, namely West Walk House built in 1983 and designed by the Winchester architect, Robert Adam. In Chapter 6, the conclusion was drawn that none of the buildings in The Close that had been considered could be regarded as Palladian. Indeed, there never was a Palladian building erected in The Close until West Walk House came along. Though clearly a modern house for modern living, and though modest in scale, the references to the villas of Palladio or to, say, Lord Burlington's design for Tottenham House are immediately apparent both in the plans and the elevations. However, the domestic feel of the building, especially the large roof, has also been influenced by the Arts and Crafts movement and the architect's drawing (fig.181) shows, in the background, Palladio and Lutyens in conversation.

Although it is over 400 years since Palladio's death in 1580, it is clear that his influence has persisted and that interest in his architectural style remains strong. The architectural revolution that Inigo Jones set in train in the 1620s not only continued, in some form or another, for another 200 years but established a recognisable style and set design standards which have influenced architectural taste to the present day. Palladianism itself became modified as the 17th and 18th centuries went on, despite the vigorous efforts of the neo-Palladians to establish it as *the* national style, and was then somewhat eclipsed during the Age of Revivals in the 19th and early 20th centuries. Then, in the face of new materials and the Modern Movement, it became no more than another historical style on a par with, say, Gothic or Egyptian. But now, such is the renewed interest in the works of the Renaissance, of great architects like Jones, Wren, Chambers and Soane as well as in the discreet, good taste of the Georgian era, that the period of discontinuity that we have gone through may now be at an end. This is not to say that Britain is about to undergo some sort of new Palladian revival. West Walk House is welcome because it draws from the spirit of Palladio without using classical motifs. The crusading and high-minded days of Modernism may be over, but it has left a legacy that makes most people very suspicious of historical detail in modern buildings. The man in the street, with any sort of interest in architecture, may well support Prince Charles's well-known views in support of traditional building methods, forms and materials but would draw the line at trying to revive 'classical architecture'.

An important example of Georgian renaissance is taking place in Bath with the Bath Spa Millennium Project. With re-furbishment of the Cross and Hot Baths and a new building where the Tepid Bath used to be, the aim is to revive the tradition of taking the waters – but with modern facilities in a mix of new and historic buildings. The new building – a cube rising within a glass frame – is intended both to echo the form of the Hot Bath and to provide it with a suitable back-drop. But, more importantly, the project will re-vitalise a corner of Bath which is presently 'dead' but which was laid out in its present form a little more than 200 years ago, solely for the purpose of making it easier and more comfortable for people to use the baths and to move about within the heart of the spa town. The function died but the form largely remained. The re-creation of the former use in a way that looks both to the future and to Bath's historic past has to be the best possible form of 'conservation'.

And looking after what we have is, indeed, the current challenge. This does not, of course, mean freezing buildings in their existing state, since owners' requirements constantly change and it is often the layers of physical change that make an old building of interest. The principal mechanism for achieving the necessary balancing act is the system of 'listing'. Once a building is listed by the Department of Environment as being of special architectural or historical interest, the owner is put on notice of the need for any work affecting the fabric or the character or setting of the building to be approved by the local planning authority. At the same time, listing can provide an entrée to any local building grants system that exists; this will normally ensure that an owner receives some financial assistance towards the cost of essential maintenance work on the building. The first grants scheme in the country was begun in Bath in 1955. (At the time of writing, grant schemes are operated by Kennet, North Wiltshire, Salisbury and West Wiltshire District Councils but not by Swindon Council nor by Bath & North East Somerset Council). By these means, work to listed buildings is normally supervised by experts from the local authority and, in appropriate cases, from English Heritage as well. However, this form of control is often only nominal since there are nowadays so many more craftsmen with the necessary skills and experience to undertake high-class repair and maintenance work on a listed building compared with, say, 30 years ago. Despite all these arrangements, there remains the risk of alterations being made to a listed building that are not only unauthorised but irreversible, though this is a diminishing risk with a wider appreciation of our heritage.

Perhaps a more serious threat at present is from the effects of air pollution – not from industrial chimneys or from domestic fireplaces but from the exhaust gases of motor vehicles. This is a special worry in Bath, where the location of the city in a natural bowl often causes the fumes to linger. The damage which this type of pollution causes, to buildings as well as people, is undoing the benefits which had been achieved under the clean air legislation from the late 1950s onwards.[4] Similar fears are starting to be expressed in Salisbury which, too, suffers from excessive traffic and is surrounded by hills. In some streets of Bradford-on-Avon, the lower parts of the street frontages of buildings faced with Bath stone are suffering from corrosion; the cause might be salt on the roads being thrown up by heavy traffic.

But to end on a happier note, and putting earlier mistakes and disasters behind us, it is probably fair to say that our architectural treasures enjoy a more secure future than they ever have. Any photographs of buildings taken more than 40 or 50 years ago will certainly show many that have disappeared but they will also show others that, compared to the same buildings today, look worn out, neglected and often ill-treated. Thanks to a more enlightened approach on the part of their owners, as well as to a host of local initiatives, Wiltshire and Bath's heritage of classical buildings should long continue to be a source of great delight.

4. See *Caring for Bath* (Bath City Council, 1995).

Glossary of Architectural Terms

Acroterion: Strictly, the blocks at the top point and the ends of a Pediment to carry an ornament but often used to include the ornament itself (pl.acroteria).

Aedicule: In classical architecture, an architectural frame for a niche or window consisting, e.g., of Pilasters supporting an engaged Pediment and often a cill (also a Tabernacle).

Antis (In): see Portico.

Arcade: A row of arches supported by piers or Columns; usually it is left open either to allow movement within a covered space or to mark its edge (as in a Loggia); but if it is an architectural feature forming part of a wall, it is called a blind arcade.

Architrave: (1) the lowest section of a classical Entablature.
(2) a door or window surround. Lugged A. – where the top of the surround projects slightly on each side. Shouldered A. – where the top end of the surround projects slightly both upwards and sideways.

Astylar: Of a classical façade, without either columns or pilasters.

Attic: In classical architecture, the upper storey of a structure above the cornice.

Bucranium: Ox skull motif used as a feature in a classical frieze.

Cartouche: A tablet in the form of a scroll for an inscription or emblem; usually oval or irregular in shape with moulded edges and a convex centre and either carved in stone or wood or part of a painting.

Coffering: A system of decorating a ceiling or vault with recessed square or polygonal units or panels.
Coffered: describes a surface so decorated.

Colonnade: A line of columns.

Column: In classical architecture, a round shaft and its capital and base (if it has one); if it is partly absorbed by a wall, it is called an Engaged Column (or sometimes Attached or Applied).

182. Coffering: New Wardour Castle

Console: An S-shaped decorative support usually with one end larger and more elaborate than the other and enriched with mouldings or leaf shapes.

Cornice: see Entablature.

Cupola: A small dome supported by a round or polygonal structure (often consisting only of columns) rising from a larger dome or a roof.

183. Console: No.54 St.Ann's Street, Salisbury, used here as a support for a door hood

Diocletian Window: A window shaped like the top half of a circle and divided into three by vertical members (or mullions); originally used in the Baths of Diocletian (also Thermae or Thermal Window).

Dressings: Stone blocks, normally smooth (or 'dressed') used for the Quoins, String Courses and door and window surrounds of a building usually to provide a contrast to other material of a different kind or colour.

Engaged Column: see Column.

Entablature: The horizontal elements of a classical order supported by the Columns. It consists (from bottom upwards) of the architrave (usually a plain or beam-like element), the frieze (in most of the Orders, containing ornamental features) and the cornice (moulded and progressively projecting).

Frieze: see Entablature.

Gauged Brickwork: (or Rubbed Brickwork) Consisting of bricks which are smoothed or rubbed down (with a hard material) to form precise edges enabling them to be laid with very fine joints of lime mortar; commonly found in the arches and lintels of doors and windows of Georgian houses.

184. Gauged (or Rubbed) brickwork: Marlborough

Greek Cross: A cruciform plan where the four arms of the cross are of equal length.

Loggia: A Colonnaded or Arcaded gallery with one or more open sides.

Metope: The square space in a Doric Frieze between two Triglyphs; it can either be decorated or left plain.

Modillion: One of a series of small brackets, in the form of a Console, often used to support a cornice (hence, a 'modillioned cornice').

Mutule: In the Doric Order, the blocks on the underside of the Cornice from which the guttae (pegs) depend (thought to derive from a system of timber building with beam ends and pegs).

Oeil de Boeuf Window: A small circular or oval window (also called Bullseye Window).

Order: (1) In classical architecture, a Column and its Entablature – but the term also implies the formality and discipline pertaining to the classical system of Orders;

(2) sometimes the term is used of the Column alone (but as part of a larger system) as in 'Giant Order', i.e. a Column rising through two or more storeys.

Palladian Window: see Venetian Window.

Patera: A round, shallow ornament often used to decorate a Metope.

Pavilion: In classical architecture, a section of a building which projects in plan from the adjoining part and usually designed to appear as a building on its own.

Pediment: (1) The triangular gable end of a classical temple (or a temple-like front as a feature of a building) with the Cornice continued round the sloping sides.
(2) A similar feature used elsewhere in a classical building e.g. above a porch, a door or a window; in such cases it may be curved at the top or its sides or its base left incomplete.

Peristyle: A range of Columns that go all around a building (or a space within a building).

Piano Nobile: The storey of a house that contains the main reception rooms usually with a ground floor, or semi-basement, below and one or more smaller storeys above.

Pilaster: A representation of a classical Column against a wall with a flat (or fluted) suface and projecting only slightly (usually one-sixth of its width) from the surface of the wall.

Pilaster Strip: A plain Pilaster without a capital or base, rarely used in classical architecture (also called a lessene).

Plat Band: see String Course.

Portico: (1) Originally, the covered entrance to a classical temple with the end of the roof (and its Pediment) supported by Columns; if it projects from the front of the temple (with Columns on three sides) it is called 'prostyle' but if the covered space is within the front of the temple it is called 'in antis';
(2) any similar arrangement in a classical building with a temple-like front, often where no actual roof (extending from front to back) exists at all;
(3) a porch – provided it has a Pediment and Columns.

Prostyle: see Portico.

Quoin: (1) (Strictly speaking) the outside corners of a wall or building;
(2) (more frequently) one of the dressed stones forming the corner, usually laid with their long and short ends alternately.

Rustic (the): A term sometimes used for the floor below the Piano Nobile usually containing service quarters and deriving its name from the fact that its outward face is often Rusticated.

Rustication: The treatment of stone-work to give the impression of strength by using distinct recessed joints.

***185**. Rustication: The Guildhall, Bath*

Segmental: The shape of a segment, i.e. part of a circle less than a semi-circle.

Serlian Window: see Venetian Window.

Spandrel: The space in one of the upper corners of a rectangular space containing an arch.

String Course: A continuous projecting horizontal band on a wall, usually between storeys; it is often decorated (e.g.with a Vitruvian Scroll) or moulded but if entirely plain is sometimes called a Plat Band.

Tabernacle: see Aedicule.

Terminal Figure (or **Term**): A pedestal tapering towards the base and usually supporting a bust.

Triglyph: The feature in a Doric frieze, consisting of three vertical bars, which alternates with the Metopes; it is a representation of the end of a beam.

186. Venetian Windows: a Wiltshire selection. (from left to right): No.24 High Street, Warminster; New Wardour Castle; St.Nicholas's Church, Hardenhuish, Chippenham; Lynchetts, Woolley Streeet, Bradford-on-Avon

Venetian Window: A window of three lights, the central one taller than the others and usually divided from them by one or more Columns (also called Serlian or, less correctly, Palladian).

Vermiculation: A method of carving the surface of a block of stone (as in Rustication) to give it the appearance of worm casts.

Vitruvian Scroll: Decoration on a String Course or Cornice in the form of a continuous series of breaking waves (also called Running Dog).

Volute: A spiral scroll which is the principal feature of an Ionic capital and an element of a Corinthian and a Composite capital.

187. Volutes of Ionic Capital: Philipps House, Dinton

Further Reading

Architecture – General

Clifton-Taylor, Alec, *The Pattern of English Building* (Batsford, London,1962; 4th edition Faber & Faber, London, 1987)

Colvin, Howard, *A Biographical Dictionary of British Architects 1600-1840* (Murray, London, 1954; new edition 1978)

Fleming, John; Honour, Hugh and Pevsner, Nikolaus, *A Dictionary of Architecture* (Penguin Books, Harmondsworth, 1966)

Pevsner, Nikolaus, *An Outline of European Architecture* (Penguin Books, Harmondsworth, 1943; 5th revised edition 1957)

Pevsner, Nikolaus, *The Buildings of England: Wiltshire* (Penguin Books, Harmondsworth, 1963; revised by Cherry, Bridget, 1975)

Pevsner, Nikolaus, *The Buildings of England: North Somerset and Bristol* (Penguin Books, Harmondsworth, 1958)

Watkin, David, *A History of Western Architecture* (Barrie & Jenkins, London, 1986; reissued Laurence King, London, 1992)

Yarwood, Doreen, *The Architecture of Britain* (Batsford, London, 1976)

Classical and Georgian Architecture – General

Adam, Robert, *Classical Architecture, A Complete Handbook* (Viking, London, 1992)

Arnold, Dana, *The Georgian Country House* (Sutton, Stroud, 1998)

Ayres, James, *Building the Georgian City* (Yale University Press, New Haven & London, 1998)

Cruickshank, Dan, *A Guide to the Georgian Buildings of Britain and Ireland* (Weidenfeld & Nicolson, London, 1985)

Curl, James Stevens, *Georgian Architecture* (David & Charles, Newton Abbot, 1993)

Mowl, Timothy and Earnshaw, Brian, *Architecture Without Kings: The Rise of Puritan Classicism under Cromwell* (Manchester University Press, Manchester, 1995)

Murray, Peter, *The Architecture of the Italian Renaissance* (Thames & Hudson, London, 1969)

Parissien, Steven, *The Georgian Group Book of the Georgian House* (Aurum Press, London, 1995)

Reid, Richard, *The Georgian House and Its Details* (Bishopsgate Press, London, 1989)

Summerson, John, *Architecture in Britain 1530-1830* (Penguin Books, Harmondsworth, 1953; 5th revised edition 1969)

Summerson, John, *The Architecture of the Eighteenth Century* (Thames & Hudson, London, 1969)

Summerson, John, *The Classical Language of Architecture* (Thames & Hudson, London, 1963; revised edition 1980)

Summerson, John, *Georgian London* (Pleiades Books, London, 1945; 2nd edition, Penguin Books, Harmondsworth, 1962)

Wittkower, Rudolf, *Architectural Principles in the Age of Humanism* (Tiranti, London, 1952; revised edition, Academy Editions, London, 1973)

Worsley, Giles, *Classical Architecture in Britain: The Heroic Age* (Yale University Press, New Haven & London, 1995)

Individual Architects

Ackerman, James, *Palladio* (Pelican Books, Harmondsworth, 1966)

Girouard, Mark, *Robert Smythson and The Elizabethan Country House* (Yale University Press, New Haven & London, 1983)

Harris, John, *Sir William Chambers* (Zwemmer, London, 1970)

Mowl, Timothy and Earnshaw, Brian, *John Wood, Architect of Obsession* (Millstream Books, Bath, 1988)

Robinson, John Martin, *The Wyatts, An Architectural Dynasty* (Oxford University Press, New York, 1979)

Stutchbury, Howard, *The Architecture of Colen Campbell* (Manchester University Press, Manchester, 1967)

Summerson, John, *Inigo Jones* (Pelican Books, Harmondsworth, 1966)

Turner, Roger, *Capability Brown and The Eighteenth Century Landscape* (Weidenfeld & Nicolson, London, 1985)

Wittkower, Rudolf, *Palladio and English Palladianism* (Thames & Hudson, London, 1974)

Individual Buildings or Locations

Gorst, Thom, *Bath, An Architectural Guide* (Ellipsis, London, 1997)

Little, Bryan, *The Building of Bath 47-1947: An Architectural and Social Study* (Collins, London, 1947)

Ison, Walter, *The Georgian Buildings of Bath* (Faber & Faber, London, 1948; reprinted, Kingsmead Press, Bath, 1980)

Jackson, Neil, *Nineteenth Century Bath, Architects and Architecture* (Ashgrove Press, Bath, 1991)

Ladd, Frederick, *Architects at Corsham Court* (Moonraker Press, Bradford-on-Avon, 1978)

Morriss, Richard and Hoverd, Ken, *The Buildings of Bath* (Alan Sutton, Stroud, 1993)

Morriss, Richard and Hoverd, Ken, *The Buildings of Salisbury* (Alan Sutton, Stroud, 1994)

Mowl, Timothy, *Palladian Bridges* (Millstream Books, Bath, 1993)

Royal Commission on Historical Monuments, *Ancient and Historical Monuments in the City of Salisbury, Volume I* (HMSO, London, 1980)

Royal Commission on Historical Monuments, *Salisbury, The Houses of the Close* (Stationery Office, London, 1993)

Royal Commission on Historical Monuments, *Wilton House and English Palladianism* (HMSO, London, 1988)

Miscellaneous

Aslet, Clive and Powers, Alan, *The National Trust Book of The English House* (Viking, London, 1985)

Jackson-Stops, Gervase, *The Country House in Perspective* (Pavilion Books, London, 1990)

Mowl, Timothy, *William Beckford, Composing for Mozart* (Murray, London, 1998)

Lees-Milne, James, *Earls of Creation* (Hamish Hamilton, London, 1962)

Index

Buildings of Wiltshire and Bath mentioned in the text are entered, where appropriate, under the town or village in which they are located. See the map on p.10 for their locations.